**Helping the Adult Survivor
of Child Sexual Abuse**

For Friends, Family & Lovers

Helping the Adult Survivor of
Child Sexual Abuse
For Friends, Family & Lovers

by Kathe Stark

Mother Courage Press
1667 Douglas Avenue
Racine, WI 53404

Copyright 1993 © by Kathe Stark. All rights reserved. No part of this publication may be reproduced, stored in a retrieval system or transmitted in any form or by any means, electronic photocopying, recording or otherwise, without the prior written permission of the publisher.

Library of Congress catalog card number 93-77709
ISBN 0-941300-26-9

Mother Courage Press
1667 Douglas Avenue
Racine, WI 53404-2721

This book is dedicated in loving memory to my father, Howard Dickey, who passed away before he could witness my healing.

Acknowledgments

First of all, I want to thank the survivors of child sexual abuse, their friends, families and lovers, for the honor of their trust, for allowing me to hear their pain and joy, to learn from them and for the pleasure of witnessing their healing.

Brian Baxter and Kris Rotter, Ph.D., encouraged me to start this project and had no doubt that I could write this book.

Gary Schoener, Laura Kuhn and Lynn B. Daugherty, Ph.D., spent many hours reading, editing and criticizing the manuscript in progress, providing insights and new ideas, suggesting invaluable sources and serving as sounding boards for ideas as I clarified and organized them.

Robert Werner, M.D., Ph.D., endured my personal struggle as a survivor and provided a safe, nurturing environment in which I could learn to trust and finally break the silence of my own secret. You will no doubt recognize in these pages much of your wisdom and spirit. You have contributed greatly to my well being, and for that I will always be grateful.

John Torseth, M.D., has provided a strong shoulder and has been loving, understanding and supportive as I struggled to learn to love and trust again.

I am especially grateful to my family who stood by my side and shared the struggle of my healing, and to Nola Weise who accepted me as I am and has never failed to provide the kind of support I needed most.

Finally, I wish to thank my publishers, Jeanne Arnold and Barbara Lindquist of Mother Courage Press, who made it possible to publish this book.

Introduction

A bachelor of arts degree in human services with an emphasis on victimization and mental health, internships as a rape and sexual assault counselor and work in the field of mental health puts some credits after my name, but none are as important as the credits I have given myself—C.S.A.S: Child Sexual Abuse Survivor. I am an expert on this topic from a very personal perspective.

Sexually abused from the age of 10 until 13 by a member of the clergy, I lived my life repeatedly finding myself in abusive situations without any knowledge of why. Finally, at the age of 33 and in the midst of yet another abusive situation, the terrors of my initial abuse came pouring back to engulf my entire life. Unable to work, sleep or eat, I entered intensive therapy and later began to study about the sexual abuse of children and its aftermath. Finally, everything in my life began to make sense.

Throughout this period of crisis and distress, friends and family would ask, "What can I do to help?" but I didn't even know how to put into words what I needed from them. After years in therapy and years of studying victimization, I am now able to put down on paper all the things I wished I could have told those around me who wanted to help with my struggle and my pain.

It is important for you to know that while I write this book from my own experience as a child sexual abuse survivor, I incorporate, as well, experiences of countless others I have met along my journey. Survivors have shared their stories with me and their support people have repeatedly asked and found answers to the question, "What can I do to help?"

This book contains background theory you will be needing if you decide to help an adult child sexual abuse victim become an adult survivor. As your loved one gets the professional help needed to become a survivor instead of a victim, you will be exposed to some theories and ideas you may not otherwise have heard before. You will need to understand what happens to children who are sexually abused, and why and how that early abuse has a lasting impact on their lives.

A small booklet entitled "Women Helping Women: Healing the Wounds of Child Sexual Abuse" that I wrote for one of my college classes was the forerunner of this project. When the booklet was completed, requests for more copies began to come in from individuals, groups, and a local bookstore. These requests confirmed what I already knew—although numerous books exist for the victim/survivor, meagre, almost hidden chapters within them were all that was available for the family, friends and lovers trying to understand.

It is my wish that this book will guide those friends, family and lovers who are involved with an adult survivor of child sexual abuse understand what has happened and is happening to the one they love so they are better able to reach out and help him or her through this struggle. It is my hope that this book will help to insure that friendships, families and intimate relationships do not dissolve under the pressure and misunderstandings about adult survivors and the struggle they must face in order to make sense of what happened to them as young, defenseless children.

It is often the wounded who are best able to help others who have been similarly wounded. Rielke wrote, "Do not believe that she who seeks to comfort you now lives untroubled among the simple and quiet words that sometimes do you good. Her life has much difficulty and sadness. Were it otherwise, she would never have been able to find those words."

I speak from experience and draw from the experiences of the friends family and lovers in this book, and I trust that I can offer strength and reassurance that a commitment to help a child sexual abuse victim become a survivor is one with uncountable rewards.

Contents

Introduction ix

Child sexual abuse, the damage 1

Helping the survivor: what does it mean? 3
    The Commitment of Helping 3
    Living deliberately 9
    Taking care of yourself 12

Child sexual abuse: the basics 15
    "The War Within" 15
    What is child sexual abuse? 15
    There's always a threat 19
    When a child is sexually abused 22
    Emotional numbing 24

Remembering: the early stage of recovery 27
    "Bad Person" 27
    "But she was fine until now" 27
    Why remember now: traumatic amnesia 33
    The healing process 37
    How can you help someone in the process of healing? 39
    The six stages of healing 40
    Remembering the past 47
    When the traumatic-amnesia survivor is remembering 49
    Encourage the child sexual abuse survivor to get help 51
    Group therapy 54
    Communication 55
    Guilt 60

    Dissociation 62
    Isolation 66
    How can you help? 68
    Post Traumatic Stress Disorder and depression 70
    Suicide: Do not ignore the signs 72
    How to act when you suspect suicide is being considered 74
    Self-Mutilation 80

The healing journey 83
    "Understanding" 83
    From victim to survivor 83
    Touch 88
    Feelings 91
    Anger 93
    Grief and mourning 99
    Anxiety 101
    Issues of control in the adult survivor 103
    Making changes 107
    Forgive and forget 113

Special topics 117
    "An Interesting Gentleman" 117
    Confrontation 118
    The actual confrontation 121
    Not for everyone 123
    Especially for lovers 124
    Therapy 128
    When the abuse was incest 130
    The split family 137
    When the abuser was a cleric 139
    Recovery?—recovered?—resolution! 144

References 151

Child sexual abuse, the damage

The individual manifestations of damage from child sexual abuse are as varied as the persons involved, but there is a certain commonality. The most common symptoms that are frequently seen as the result of child sexual abuse are
- Very low self-esteem
- Immense sense of shame and guilt
- Feelings of helplessness, powerlessness
- Difficulty with intimacy of any sort
- An inability to trust
- Hypersensitivity to touch
- A drive toward perfection in everything the victim undertakes
- Emotional unresponsiveness or emotional numbing
- Self-defeating and self-destructive behaviors
- Symptoms of severe depression and Post Traumatic Stress Disorder (PTSD)

These symptoms may be manifested in ways that can be very subtle or ways that obviously indicate something is terribly wrong.

While males as well as females are sexually abused as children, the majority of sexual abuse is perpetrated against females. I have taken the liberty, in most cases, of referring to the victim/survivor with the female pronoun.

Helping the survivor: what does it mean?

The Commitment of Helping

Since survivors and their symptoms are so diverse, there is no single model to indicate the "right" way to help. But when we can truly help someone heal, we contribute to the nurturing and growth of another human being. As a benefit, we feel good about ourselves. We enjoy a sense of worth and joy as we see someone we love, who has been struggling to live and grow, send out new shoots and begin to reach toward the warmth of the sun. We can help the victim battle the memories of child sexual abuse and restore the gift of hope to the survivor.

Deciding to help a friend, family member or lover heal from child sexual abuse is a commitment that will truly change your life, even though the focus is on helping her or him. Before entering into this commitment, it is critical for both you and your loved one to comprehend, as fully as possible, what this will mean to you. The real-life experiences of those in this book who have undertaken this task, in retrospect, speak of their commitment as one of the most painful and most rewarding experiences they have ever made to another person. One of the major themes of this book is truth; therefore, a concerted effort is made here to speak the truth about such a commitment—its positive and negatives. The negatives may frighten you or cause you to reconsider, but the experiences of others can offer strength and reassurance that this commitment is one with uncountable rewards.

First, you need to know that the commitment is one of time. Time will be spent listening, providing support, offering encouragement, helping to get professional help or other support. How long and how often will you spend time with the victim or on the telephone with her? There is no mathematical formula to advise how much time will be involved. The choice is yours alone. Each individual interviewed for this book spoke definitively of a large time commitment, particularly in the early stages of consciously remembering when each memory may bring with it a fresh wave of pain, depression and crisis. You may be on-call 24 hours a day, particularly if the victim has no other sources of support. In one very striking example, the victim's sister and her husband decided early on that it would be in the best interest of everyone's health and safety if the victim moved in with them during the initial period of crisis. This is not to suggest that this is the solution for everyone, but for this couple and the victim the arrangement proved to be the best choice for each of them.

The commitment of time is often long term. In the early stages of remembering, the time you spend is likely to be frequent, for long durations, intense and with the potential for many crises. This stage is not time limited. Once it begins, there is no method to predict its course. For some it may be a matter of months, for others a year or more. Regardless of duration, it is the stage during which the survivor needs the most support. This is truly the beginning of healing. Strong support during this time provides the survivor with the courage to continue on a journey that may be very frightening for her.

As the survivor moves into healing and resolution, your time commitment may decrease in frequency and duration, but it remains extremely important as the survivor relearns to trust, as she feels well enough to begin to emerge socially, and as she begins to formulate plans and make decisions about her future. At this point, you are the one who has been with her through the most difficult time and, as a result, she has come to depend and trust you implicitly and will seek out your suggestions and opinions.

The commitment of time you make to help an adult survivor is both short and long term in a very relative sense. It can range from months to years and varies in intensity, depending upon the stage of healing the individual is in and the other support available to her. Whatever your particular situation, you should know that the time commitment involved is substantial and requires consistency.

Only you can decide if you are ready for such a commitment. It is extremely important if you choose to proceed, that you are also prepared to see it all the way through. The effects on the victim if she looses the one person she has trusted with her horrible secret and inner-most feelings before she has attained her health can be devastating. As a child victim, your loved one felt the deepest pain of betrayal by an adult who was trusted by her. The loss of your commitment midway in the healing process may bring back all of those feelings of betrayed trust at a time when the individual is very sensitive and emotionally vulnerable.

Contemplate seriously the time you feel prepared to invest and then make that commitment with the same type of significance you attach to your wedding vows. There will be good times and bad but, if you love and cherish this bruised and wounded person, you and she will reap the rewards of your commitment. You will see and experience her positive change and growth, her deep, personal healing.

Your commitment is also one to pain. It is a commitment that exposes you to the pain of the abused individual for whom you deeply care. It is a commitment which may envelop you in her pain and may touch a personal pain within yourself that you have been unaware of. We are not robotic machines capable of hearing or observing intense pain without an emotional response. We are human beings whose wondrous capabilities include being able to not only hear and see another's pain but to actually feel it within ourselves, to experience true empathy for another.

As one family member put it, "I felt like I was right down there in the muck with her—feeling my sister's unbearable pain from which neither of us could escape and I could not separate myself from."

Remembering that through pain comes the opportunity for growth and that the pain does not last forever will give way to hope can be a comfort during rough times. The rewards of experiencing another's pain in her healing journey, with the knowledge that it signals growth, can provide the strength to continue the commitment to support.

If you are a family member in support of an incest survivor, very strong personal pain may abe unavoidable but it can become a part of your helping process. In the majority of incestuous families it is the father who was the perpetrator, the same father who may never have laid a hand on you. This is not unusual. Often only one child is chosen within the family to be the victim. Being a part of your sibling's pain, as he/she struggles with the recollection and trauma of the sexual abuse at the hands of your father, in *your* house, is likely to raise numerous issues of your own pain. Questions that may have no immediate answers: Why not you? Did you know what going on? If you did, why didn't you tell anyone? Suddenly coming face-to-face with issues such as these can unleash a powerful inner pain best dealt with by seeking your own professional counselor to help clarify where the survivor's issues end and yours begin. You can't continue as an effective helper if you attempt to disguise your personal pain and its accompanying feelings of guilt. Disguising that part of yourself will render you an emotional cripple on this issue, unable to help your brother or sister. A professional can assist you to learn how to experience your pain separately and to seek answers to your own questions. This can enable you to resume your commitment to your sibling's healing.

The commitment you make must be absolute acceptance of your loved one. Acceptance that the secret of abuse being shared with you now is the absolute truth to be believed and validated, never questioned. And in the case of sibling incest, this is even more important. Even if you lived within the same house with the victim of incest, you may have never known what was occurring. No matter how much you would now like to believe that you knew everything, you didn't and you couldn't have. To make the commitment to help is to admit that you don't possess all knowledge about the family you shared. This acceptance frees you so you are able to unconditionally accept the survivor, who may seek many things from you, but the most feverishly sought is your unconditional acceptance of her, of what happened to her, and of who she is right now as a result of all that occurred.

This commitment may mean acting as an advocate for the survivor. This may be especially true if the criminal justice system is going to become involved. In several states new legislation has been enacted which allows the survivor of child sexual abuse to file charges against the abuser years after the actual abuse occurred. Your state's attorney general's office can advise you about the laws in your state. The legal process and system can be very frightening, and the survivor may need your help and support navigating through it.

You can act as an advocate in other ways as well. If the survivor is temporarily unable to continue her employment, help her to seek out available disability benefits. You can also act as the survivor's advocate with friends and family members who don't understand or don't want to understand what is happening to their loved one. This may mean accompanying the survivor to various functions when she may have contact with these individuals. It may also entail acting on behalf of the survivor during times that the added stress of being with people who don't understand may be too stressful and be harmful to her.

This commitment to support a survivor is one of trust. It is a commitment to shed all pretense in order to see and feel that which was and is. It may mean the dismantling of an old system of protective denial that has hidden the truth and held the traumatic past at bay. The truth becomes the key to unlock the potential for living a full life possible for the first time, a life with the solid knowledge and acceptance of the "I" that is the survivor. The old masks of pretense used in defense of the "I" become no longer a necessary layer of protection between the survivor and the world because with truth comes the knowledge that "I" can exist and survive. "I" can be conscious and have pain but not be devoured by that pain.

The commitment is one to truth—a giving up all pretense. This means to eradicate those seemingly harmless lies told everyday to "protect" the feelings of others, the lies which essentially protect no one but ourselves, but which can result in further damage to the victim in their quest to re-learn how to trust.

> *Camille recalled how her husband suddenly took up jogging as her trauma unfolded. Many times she tried to tell him she understood that he needed time apart from her and an activity that could release his own pent-up emotions. Each time he declined to acknowledge any association between his newly found sport and the drama being played out in their lives.*
>
> *Camille found this pretense fueled her inner feeling that she was still a victim, that her husband was trying to protect her from his real feelings because she would be unable to handle them. She felt this identified her as a victim unable to take care of herself.*
>
> *In contrast, dropping the pretense carries the message that, while the truth may bring with it some deep hurt, "I feel I can share it with you because I have confidence in you, and together we can see it through."*

The commitment is one to confront conflict. When child sexual abuse is reported by the adult survivor, it is not uncommon for lines of allegiance to be drawn among friends and family. This is no more clearly evident than in an incestuous family where disbelievers side with the perpetrator, to the complete exclusion of the survivor, and believers align themselves with the survivor. This same dynamic occurs when the sexual abuse has occurred outside of the family. In either case, such divisions indicate conflicts that can be on-going and taxing to everyone involved. Conflicts that must be confronted if you are committed to supporting the survivor.

Your commitment to help the survivor may involve you in conflicts. This is particularly true if you are a family member or close friend of the family, and it may be an extremely difficult experience for you. Believing the survivor often means giving up close ties to others—a loss that you need to consider. You can't have it both ways and help the survivor. The survivor's trust is badly damaged and a close, helping relationship with you would be extremely difficult, if not impossible, if you remain aligned with both sides of the split family. The survivor needs to feel absolute trust in you from the start. Your commitment must include the potential for conflict you may experience between the survivor, her family and friends—conflict with those who do not choose to try to understand and accept the survivor or those who would rather ignore what has happened to the survivor in the past, as well as what is happening to her now.

If this commitment to help an adult survivor sounds difficult, that is because it is. But out of commitment can come such wonderful rewards. Those who shared their experiences for this book all agreed that they were happy they decided to be integral part of the healing process.

> *"I saw Sharon move from a limp pile of raw nerves, tears and fears to a woman who stands tall, confident in her deepest self. I felt so proud to have played my small part in this remarkable growth and recovery by being there for her."*

> *"I felt Karen's pain go right through me and touch a vulnerable spot inside I thought was long healed. Together*

we grew beyond our pain and to become better people because of it."

"When Dennis first told me his secret I wanted to shout "liar" not because I didn't believe him but because the truth of what my husband had done to him was too much for me to bear. I wallowed in my own pain and guilt for a while, but I looked up long enough to see the devastation engulfing my son and knew I had to be there for him. We still have periods of pain, but now we know we can always share them."

Living deliberately

To be the adult survivor of child sexual abuse or to be the friend, family member or lover providing the survivor support, understanding and love during these turbulent times requires that each of you live your lives deliberately. To live deliberately requires forethought, planning, choosing alternatives and sometimes rehearsing responses to situations. The survivor may have already turned the corner from viewing herself as a victim to seeing herself as a survivor, but that view may still be rather tentative and needs to be continually strengthened. To live deliberately provides the survivor with the time and experience necessary to add "tenacity" to her belief that "I *am* a survivor rather than a victim."

The use of an example illustrates what it means to live deliberately.

Marcy was repeatedly sexually abused by her alcoholic father beginning at the age of seven and ending when she turned twelve. Her two younger sisters have no recollection of any abuse at all. Mary Lee responded to Marcy's recollection of the abuse with absolute disbelief and has completely rejected her. Katie believed without question that Marcy was abused and has been her main source of support through all of the remembering, the crisis periods, the fits of anger and now into early resolution.

All received an invitation to attend the graduation and open house of a niece they are very fond of. Marcy felt she had only one choice—to decline the invitation because her father and mother would be there. This was a confrontation she neither wanted nor felt ready to have. But together the sisters worked out an alternative. To live deliberately in this situation opened the doors to options other than declining the invitation. It provided a means to attend and enjoy the graduation while simultaneously ensuring a high level of safety and comfort for the survivor.

Here's how it worked for Marcy.

- Marcy and Katie agreed that Marcy should not go alone to the graduation nor go unprepared. Katie agreed to accompany her, both as her sister and as a source of moral support.
- Marcy then asked for the help of a close supportive friend Jan. Katie couldn't possibly spend all of her time at Marcy's side with her own two small children to care for. Jan agreed to attend the graduation.
- Marcy, Katie and Jan rehearsed numerous possible situations that might arise at the graduation. These rehearsals provided Marcy with an opportunity to expect the worst and decide on the action she would take to prevent feeling revictimized.
- An important element of the plan was for Katie and Jan to act as supplemental "eyes and ears" for Marcy. They would pay attention to where her father was in order to alert Marcy so she could move to a different location and avoid a confrontation.

This is one example of living deliberately. It involves the realistic appraisal of the survivor's wants and needs, seeking the assistance of others to meet those needs, rehearsing and planning to lessen the risk involved and, finally, implementing the plan. Living deliberately does not leave everything up to chance. For the survivor in early recovery, the risks involved when dealing with chance can be devastating, and progress made can be significantly eroded in an instant.

Living deliberately includes the survivors' friends, family and lovers as well as the survivors themselves. In making your initial commitment to caring and supporting your loved one, you may undertake a long-term relationship full of tremendous pain with small, tenuous steps forward toward healing and steps backwards as well. The relationship the two of you have, or are developing, is unlike any that has preceded it. All decisions that you make that are related to the abuse issue will have an effect on the survivor and need to be acknowledged. Truth, absent of all pretense, is a critical element of living deliberately.

Marcy did not want *any* relationship with her father. Nor did she want to continue a relationship with her mother. Because of her mother's denial of Marcy's charges of the sexual abuse, she was seen as an accomplice—as guilty as her father. Katie, on the other hand, saw her mother as pathetic, aging and, while not condoning her actions surrounding the abuse, she had a desire to maintain some limited relationship with her mother. If Marcy views Katie's continued relationship with their mother as a betrayal of the trust she has established in Katie, this perception of betrayal may be experienced very much like that of the original betrayal and trauma of the abuse by her father.

Living deliberately involves choices. To live deliberately here involves making choices that create the least potential of additional trauma for the survivor, but that also takes into consideration Katie's desire to continue to see her mother. Katie honestly and deliberately discussed her position with Marcy. She emphasized that her continuing to see their mother did not lessen her commitment to Marcy, represent a betrayal of her trust or condone their mother's denial of Marcy's abuse. Through their honest efforts to communicate with each other, Marcy came to understand Katie's needs as well as clarifying her own. The resulting understanding provided room within their relationship for Katie's commitment to Marcy as well as her relationship with their mother. It is not difficult to see the potential for strong emotional turmoil for Marcy if these active steps to live deliberately were not taken.

Living deliberately means never assuming that the survivor will not find out about sensitive relationships you may choose to continue. If Katie had failed to discuss with Marcy her decision to continue a relationship with her mother for fear that it would upset Marcy, and planned secretive meetings with her mother, the likelihood is that Marcy would have discovered the secret.

These examples illustrate the importance of living deliberately as the friend, family member or lover of an adult sexual abuse survivor. Having had her trust so deeply betrayed at a young age by child sexual abuse, the adult survivor is very sensitive to similar feelings of betrayal.

Living deliberately entails living so your needs and those of the survivor can be met if you take the chance to be honest. Activities which recall old traumas for the survivor can be discussed straightforwardly to avoid painful surprises capable of impacting upon the survivor with such force that they precipitate a regression from survivor back to victim.

All of the victims and survivors interviewed for this book echoed a similar sentiment, "We [survivors] may be vulnerable at times and often feel threatened, but we are capable adults, able to discuss these fears and to come to solutions if we're given the chance."

Taking care of yourself

Making the commitment to help the adult survivor heal is one of tremendous personal time and energy. If you fail during this demanding time to allocate some time and space that is just for you and no one else, you will exhaust yourself before the goal of resolution has been achieved by the survivor. Remember, you cannot be everything to everybody all of the time without first being somebody for yourself.

The commitment to help your loved one is not a commitment to be available for every ripple of a crisis or to take care of every need that arises. There needs to be healthy limits that only you can set for yourself. Communicate those needs to the survivor and respect those personal limits. If you try to exceed personal limits, a wave of resentment may begin to grow, and it can diminish the value of what you have already done to help the survivor in the healing journey.

- Set your limits
- Communicate them to your loved one
- Advise your loved one when you are getting close to your limits

These steps keep both of you apprised and provide an opportunity for alternate plans to be made when necessary or desired.

Support groups for friends, family and lovers of adult survivors are on the increase across the country as the recognition grows that for every victim there is someone trying to help who is also in need of support and help. To locate such groups for yourself, contact any human services agency in your area or an agency that specializes in sexual assault services. These agencies maintain listings of services available to the community and can provide you with referrals. The important thing is to know in advance who can help you if the going gets tough.

The stress you feel at times while helping the survivor may lead you to believe that *you* need professional help. Dealing with the pain of a survivor who is trying to heal the deep wounds of abuse is difficult and you, too, deserve a place where you can express your own fears, frustrations and pain. A professional can assist you in developing ways to process the pain you witness without being consumed by it. Short-term professional help may assist you to sort out your own feelings about the abuse and may also help you to be a more effective supporter for your loved one.

One woman reported that seeing a therapist for a short time not only helped her address and deal with her own feelings surrounding her friend's struggle but also greatly increased her understanding of how complex that struggle really is and why. Each of us needs someone to share our inner-most thoughts and feelings with. Your loved one has you for support. As a helper, you deserve someone to fill the same role for you. If you feel that a professional counselor is what you need, seek one out. Seeking professional help for yourself is not a sign of weakness but one of strength in recognizing that you need help.

Don't stop living your life. If you golf on Saturdays or play poker on Fridays, continue to do so. Despite all of the upheaval and trauma that surrounds you, you can't place your life on hold expecting to pick it up later after this period of distress has passed. If you do, time will pass and you'll find yourself full of resentment. You may feel you always have to be available for your loved one on the chance there may be a crisis to be dealt with, but alternative arrangements can be made.

John was scheduled for a two-day fishing outing and was ready to cancel his reservation because his wife was having a very difficult time. He spoke to her therapist who advised him to go for his own well-being. The therapist suggested that a friend could spend sometime with his wife while he was gone and that the therapist would be available by telephone in the case of an emergency.

John went on the trip and while he felt guilty a bit at first, he was soon able to relax and enjoy himself. "When I came back I felt stronger, more able to stand by my wife and help her through these very difficult times. I saw what a survivor she really was. She made it through the weekend alone. We celebrated her courage that night over Chinese take-out."

John's solution is a good example of the benefits of self-care. The fishing trip provided time out for him and also gave him the opportunity to feel a sense of renewal to help his wife in her struggle.

The helping process can be very long. Without time away to refresh yourself, you will run out of the energy and strength needed to continue supporting the one you love. Give yourself some time off but remember to reassure your loved one that you are not abandoning her. Share with her your need to recharge. Then take a day and do something you enjoy; take a long walk, indulge yourself in a long bath, or work out your frustrations on the tennis court. You need and deserve time for yourself in the midst of the painful healing process of your loved one. You will be unable to help her if you ignore your own needs for very long. These can be difficult times. If you give up your own life in the name of helping your loved one you, too, will end up feeling victimized.

Child sexual abuse: the basics

The War Within
Disconnected,
> Defeated,
>> Disappointed,

Everything begins to look different.

Alone, like a child, I fear the dark.
> Both the external world
>> and the internal world are places of danger.

Panic, anger, insecurity, lost innocence.
> Bending to the will of the past,

I remain in a world which is familiar.
> Uncomfortable?
>> Yes, yet familiar.

The war within continues
> As I try to find some balance
>> Disconnected and defeated.

What is child sexual abuse?

When randomly polled, eighty out of one hundred people responded to this question with the answer that child sexual abuse always involved sexual intercourse between an adult and a child. Their answers were not entirely incorrect, but they were incomplete. To be prepared to commit oneself to helping an adult survivor heal the deep wounds of child sexual abuse, it is imperative that a more complete understanding of the various forms of child sexual abuse be accepted. Understanding that child sexual abuse is not merely one behavior but a collection of sexual behaviors perpetrated upon children will help you to comprehend the diverse reactions manifested among various adult survivors.

David Finkelhor, nationally known for his research and study in the area of child sexual abuse, provides the following definition of child sexual abuse. "Child sexual abuse is a betrayal of trust involving overt or covert sexual actions, direct or indirect, physical or verbal, which may include—but is not limited to—intercourse between a child and a trusted adult or authority figure."

The abuser may be a parent, a step-parent, a relative, a baby-sitter, a teacher, a member of the clergy or any other person in whom the child has learned to trust. Child sexual abuse is the crushing betrayal of this innocent trust.

Several important elements of child sexual abuse arise from Finkelhor's definition.

- Child sexual abuse always involves a differential in power between a child and an adult or, in the case of abuse by on older sibling, uncle or friend not yet considered an adult, a more powerful person.
- Child sexual abuse always involves the betrayal of trust a child has placed in the adult person.
- Child sexual abuse includes overt, covert, direct, indirect, physical and verbal sexual actions between the child and adult.

A partial list of child sexual abuse behavior follows.

Covert (Emotional)	**Overt (Physical)**
Household voyeurism (leering, watching children undress)	French kissing
	Fondling
Disrespecting privacy needs	Sexual hugs
Ridiculing developing bodies	Intercourse
Lewd reading to children	Sodomy
Pornography around the house	Penetration with objects
Use of objectifying, sexualizing language	Fellatio

This is not an exhaustive list but it shows that when we speak about child sexual abuse, we speak about a complex set of behaviors, used singly or in clusters, by an adult authority figure against a child. This power differential between the adult, or stronger person, and the child definitely includes the physical size and strength difference, but it also includes other factors that should not be overlooked.

The power of trust. Most child sexual abuse occurs with adult figures the child knows and trusts. The child formerly placed this trust in the adult as a person who was someone to listen to, follow and obey. A child may have no sense of impending harm when the abuser begins the seduction.

The power of dependency. In incestuous families, the largest concentration of child sexual abuse cases, the child is completely dependent upon the adult for her most basic needs, for unconditional love and for nurturing. Even in abuse that occurs outside of the family, there is a dependency by the child upon the adult. The child may depend on a scout leader or teacher to provide praise and motivation. The child may depend on a clergy member to be highly moral, even godlike, and to provide spiritual instruction and guidance. Even a next-door neighbor is depended upon to be friendly and, as an adult in the community, to be the child's protector. Contemplating the use of power this way points out that survivors may suffer emotional, physical, psychological and sexual abuse.

All these dimensions are extremely damaging to the young child and must be considered whenever we think or speak of the sexual abuse of children. *All forms of emotional, physical, psychological and sexual abuse lead to the devastation of young lives developmentally unprepared to enter into sexual relations.*

With this in mind, it should not come as a surprise that child sexual abuse is not only about sex. Child sexual abuse, like adult rape, is an act of power, capitalizing on the power differential that pre-exists between adult and child. Sex may merely be the mechanism used by the abuser to exercise power over the child. Child sexual abuse may be about sex, violence, power or any combination of these elements.

As child victims mature, it is not difficult to identify the underlying cause of their pervasive sense of powerlessness, a powerlessness that developed in childhood and continues into adulthood. This powerlessness without intervention, may manifest itself in poor intrapersonal and interpersonal relations, fears and phobias, self-destructive behaviors, addictive disorders, eating disorders and many, many more maladaptive coping mechanisms that stem from the abuse. All the survivor's manifestations are futile efforts to reclaim the power of a child lost at the point of the abuse—as unhealthy as these may appear to those outside the world of the sexually abused. If viewed in these terms, such behaviors will be seen less frequently as deviant or sick and more as natural, primitive mechanisms employed by the child, adolescent or adult to survive the traumatic breach of power and trust.

Child sexual abuse does not happen to only a few unfortunate children. Though considered by many to be substantially underestimated, the figures in this country are that one out of every three girls and one out of every seven boys are sexually abused before the age of 18. Sexual abuse is not constrained within any societal boundaries. It happens to children in every class, culture, race and religion. Abusers are fathers, step-fathers, brothers, uncles, grandparents, neighbors, teachers, baby-sitters, clergy and strangers. Although women do abuse children, the vast majority of abusers are heterosexual men.

The most important point to understand is that <u>*all*</u> *sexual abuse damages the child at a very deep inner level, and the trauma of the abuse does not end when the abuse ceases to occur.* The abused child is highly likely to experience long-term effects which, without good professional help, are carried forward into adulthood and affect his/her daily functioning in numerous ways.

The severity of the abuse cannot be assessed by the nature of the abuse incurred. The degree of violation is determined only by the feelings of the child/adult in her mind, body and spirit. If the abuse did not include forcing the child to perform oral or genital sex acts, it does not mean that the child was not violated. As seen from the previous list of abusive activities, child sexual abuse can occur without any physical contact, but that does not mean there was no violation or damage to the child. For instance, if the doors within the house were removed and the victim's abuser leeringly watched her bathe, use the toilet and dress, child sexual abuse has occurred and the child was violated.

Sexual abuse cannot be defined in terms of the length of time of involvement either. A child sexually fondled even once has been sexually abused, even as the child sexually fondled over a period of five years, and both have been damaged by the experience. *Child sexual abuse is abuse, whether it is a single occurrence or on-going situation, and neither is reducible by the other.*

In addressing child sexual abuse, comparisons are meaningless. Whether you measure the frequency, type of abuse, the abuser, or the duration of the abuse, you can never measure or make comparisons of the pain suffered by one child with that of another at the time of the actual abuse or on-going pain in the adult life of the survivors.

The adult survivor may be totally determined to heal herself, but this is a very difficult task to accomplish. Keeping the secret of the abuse is a great burden and the burden of secrecy adds to the damage incurred by the survivor. An attempt to heal alone with such a deep secret perpetuates the lonely silence and renders healing difficult, if not impossible. It is essential that the survivor have at least one person with whom she can share her secret, share the pain and share her healing.

It is my hope that this brief overview of child sexual abuse will begin to prepare you for the task you are committing to—the healing of a life. I suggest you read as much as you can on the subject for a better understanding. For more references on child sexual abuse and more in depth studies, check out the bibliography in the back of this book.

There's always a threat

If you find yourself asking, *"Why didn't the victim tell anyone about her sexual abuse until now? After all, this happened 15-20 years ago?"* you are not alone in your query. In the next section we will look at how the important elements of shame, guilt and sometimes even traumatic amnesia play vital roles in the victim's silence.

There is another important reason the victim didn't tell anyone about the abuse at the time—the threat made against the child by the perpetrator. *There is always a threat.*

The child's commitment to keep the sexual abuse a secret is strengthened by the threat of the abuser, although its form and tone may vary widely. Common associations with the word "threat" may include bodily injury, mutilation/torture, or murder. An abuser may use any of these to silence the victim from revealing what has occurred, but these threats are not the only threats used, nor are they the threats most frequently used by perpetrators. Just as insidious and effective are the types of threats that attack the inner core of the young child—the extreme vulnerability that is a natural part of childhood.

> Claire was the oldest of three girls and the incestuous relationship with her father began at the age of seven. After the first episode, her father looked her in the eye and said, "If you tell anyone about our little secret here, I'll have to do the same thing to your sisters."
>
> His threat was effective in silencing Claire and placed a heavy burden on such a young child. Claire felt that she, and she alone, was responsible for the safety of her younger sisters. Claire's father went on to abuse one of her sisters anyway but Claire still believes to the present time that she caused her own abuse and that of her sister even though she never spoke a word about the abuse to anyone—she never broke the secret.

Other effective threats survivors report that wound the inner child often include

- **Threats to remove all love from the child:** "If you tell anyone about our little secret, I'll never love you again."
- **Threats to the child's integrity:** "If you tell anyone, I'll tell them you're lying. Who do you think they'll believe, you or me?"
- **Threats to the child's sense of self:** "If you tell anyone our secret, I'll have to tell them how bad you really are and no one will ever love you again."

These less violent forms of threatening the child are often more problematic to the adult survivor because she may tend to minimize the impact of the actual threat since it did not involve a threat of bodily harm.

A survivor often fails to recognize how important the love and affection of adults is to a young developing child. Others in the survivor's life may also tend to minimize the threats that did not include physical harm. These threats must be considered from the child's perspective. From the child's viewpoint, the statements were extremely threatening and very effective.

Consider the developmental stage of the child. If Mom, Dad, or another significant adult in her life will no longer love her if she reveals the "secret," what will happen to her? Who will love and take care of her? The child is completely dependent upon this love, and both the direct and indirect threat that love will be lost is so terrifying to the young child that she often remains quiet about the abuse at the time and over the years to come.

These insidious threats are very effective at silencing the young victim because the threat is implanted so deeply and at such a young age that it becomes a part of the core beliefs held by the victim. Should the abuser die or move far away, and the threat itself cannot be carried out, its message often lives on. The messages of inner-badness, of feeling responsible for an abused sibling, the promise of rejection by those the victim loved most and numerous others live on in the mind of the victim as a reality of the consequences she will have to bear should she ever reveal the truth.

The point to be made here is that to break the silence and tell someone the secret of the childhood abuse can be extremely frightening because the threats to the child victim live on as beliefs in the adult. *It requires extreme strength and courage to break the silence of child sexual abuse at any stage of life.*

Further damage and personal devastation ensues if the victim breaks the silence and is met with disbelief, rejection or reproach. The wounds of the abuse have been inflicted and left deep scaring. To respond to the victim in ways other than to listen, believe and validate, negate both her story and her as a worthy, loveable person. It serves only to strengthen the original threat and to reopen the old wounds of the abuse and its threat of dire consequences. It is essential to recognize that in child sexual abuse there are always threats, some more hideous than others, but threats nonetheless that are very real to a young child, threats so powerful that they follow the child into adult life. With this in mind, the victim's breaking the silence can more clearly be seen as an act of courage and one deserving of your unconditional belief, validation and support.

When the survivor is able to break her long-held silence about her abuse to you, all that has been secret and hidden for a long time slowly becomes less dangerous. When you are able to listen to her painful story and validate her completely, you are sending her a clear message that her feelings are just and valid. This validation and acceptance of her story, her pain and her humanity diminishes the old threat that has held her an emotional captive for years. Reducing the powerful hold of the abuser's threat given to a small child is the first essential step toward resolution. Once the secret is broken, the survivor no longer needs to keep her secret because of fear.

When a child is sexually abused

There is one thing certain: children are never ready for sex. They are neither physically or psychologically prepared to engage in this adult activity. When it is forced upon them, significant damage is done both physically and emotionally.

To understand the damage of child sexual abuse, consider the developmental tasks involved in childhood. Each task forms the foundation or building block for the following task or stage. Failure to complete each stage or disruption of traumatic proportions within a stage can result in difficulties and disorders that carry into adulthood. This is where child sexual abuse does its greatest damage to the child victim.

Briefly noting the first four developmental tasks for children from birth to pre-adolescence will help clarify the connections between the major issues faced by the adult survivor and the consequences that the interruption of necessary stages of development have on survivors.

The first task confronting a child is to achieve a healthy level of trust. Completely dependant upon others to meet his/her needs, the child requires the development of a relationship in which she can obtain what she needs on a consistent basis. When consistent, reliable care is provided, the child develops trust in her world. If the child's needs are not met or if sexual abuse occurs, the child develops a sense of mistrust in all that is around her. This lack of trust is very frequently seen in those who have been sexually abused as children and is carried into adulthood.

The second task for each child is to develop autonomy. Having formed a trusting relationship, usually with the child's parents, the child feels confident to become separate, autonomous from them. For the child who is being sexually abused, there is no autonomy. There is no opportunity to decide on his/her own behavior and develop her own judgments; the adult abuser has taken over. The failure to develop autonomy, coupled with the sexual, abuse results in shame. Shame can be devastating for anyone, but it's particularly difficult for young children struggling for a sense of autonomy while being abused. This shame also follows the child into adulthood.

The third task is initiative. With autonomy in hand, the child is ready to undertake constructive activities on his/her own. He/she engages in all sorts of activities with great pride but this is also a time of guilt for children. They may come to feel their activity has evil consequences and experience extreme guilt associated with that activity. When the child's initiative is pre-empted by an abusing adult, the child feels the sexual activity is the activity producing evil consequences and deep feelings of guilt. Children are not yet developmentally able to separate the "bad" activity from themselves as a participant and they begin to think of themselves as "bad."

The fourth task is industry. The child wants and needs to learn the skills that characterize the adults in their lives. If the child is in an abusive family, his/her role models are very poor. Attempts to emulate adult behavior are often met with ridicule, leaving the child to feel inferior and worthless. If the abuser is in the home, the child may meet with heavy reprimand and rejection as he/she emulates the abusive behavior he/she has learned with a sibling.

To clarify the impact the interference with the developmental tasks may have on a child being sexually abused, recall the analogy of building blocks cited at the beginning of this section. Each developmental task forms the foundation block for the next, and so on. When each healthy block supports another, by the time a child comes of age, there is a healthy person ready to undertake the special tasks of adulthood. In contrast, the abused child develops on a unstable base where trust has been damaged or destroyed, autonomy has not been allowed, initiative has been taken from him/her and industry is non evident.

In summary, keep in mind that
- The damage of child sexual abuse goes much deeper than any sexual act.
- The damage of child sexual abuse goes back to the basic developmental tasks of each individual child.
- Effective healing must also go back and work to heal these early developmental issues and this takes time.
- The damage, even as deep as it is, can be healed.

Emotional numbing

For a healthy adult who knows the daily experiences of pleasure, pain, sexual fantasy and anger, to contemplate a day or a life devoid of all of these emotional sensations is extremely difficult. For the adult survivor of child sexual abuse, this lack of emotional feeling is frequently a way of life. Some would more appropriately term it as a way of non-life since to be fully alive is to experience each moment physically, cognitively and emotionally.

This emotional numbing begins with the experience of sexual abuse. As a child, the young victim is unequipped to handle what is happening to him/her physically, cognitively or emotionally. The ground swell of emotions is too intense for the small child to handle and many of the emotions are in conflict with others, creating a inner world of chaos. She may love the perpetrator but concurrently feel intense hatred toward him. She has trusted this person and now feels the deepest sense of betrayal. She has believed this individual would never hurt her and yet now she is filled with indescribable pain at the abuser's hands.

An adult experiencing such overwhelming inner conflict would feel substantial inner upheaval and stress. It would take some time for an adult to sort everything out, but it would be a task she is developmentally better prepared for. However, for the child who lacks the coping mechanisms of an adult, the emotional confusion and pain is too overwhelming; her solution is to become emotionally numb, she does this completely without conscious awareness. The child is able to stop the pain of the abuse and its aftermath only by becoming emotionally numb to it.

Emotional numbing is intended to filter out and numb the pain surrounding the abuse; however, it does not discriminate.

Emotionally numbing the pain also tends to numb pleasure, numbing the sadness also numbs excitement. Emotional numbing permeates into other emotional areas until the victim may be left with few if any emotional sensations that are not numbed to her experience. Pleasure experienced from spending time with someone may be overridden by the fear that this person will ultimately cause her pain. As a means of protection against this potential pain, emotional pleasure is numbed. A sexual fantasy creating a sexual desire may be blocked because of its painful unconscious association with the trauma of the abuse—the association that sex is bad and dirty—and may be accompanied by the victim feeling she is "bad" for having such thoughts. The warm caring feeling of being with someone the survivor is beginning to trust may be numbed because the betrayal of trust as a child victim is anticipated again within this current relationship.

Any emotion can be numbed and for some victims the numbing is extensive. Asking individuals who have not experienced sexual abuse how they feel at a given time generally does not create a dilemma in arriving at a response. For the adult child sexual abuse survivor, however, the answer may be outside of her conscious awareness. Quite literally she doesn't know how she feels. She may try and express herself using metaphors or by describing actions, but she is unable to verbalize her *feelings* which are truly unknown to her because of emotional numbing.

As the friend, family member or lover of an adult survivor, the role you can play in helping the survivor overcome her emotional numbing is a significant one.

- First, you can create an atmosphere where it is safe for the survivor to have and to express her feelings. This includes showing your own feelings and talking to the survivor about them.
- Second, you can let the survivor know that you accept her and all of her feelings unconditionally. Let her know that you will not judge or reject her because of anything she may feel or express to you.
- Third, you can encourage the survivor to express whatever she may feel to you and then demonstrate your unconditional acceptance of her and her feelings.

Overcoming this protective mechanism of emotional numbing requires trust, time and a safe supportive environment for the survivor. The joy for you and the survivor comes when he/she is first able to experience and express an emotion that emerges as a new experience after having been locked away for so many years. (See the section on Feelings.)

Remembering:
the early stage of recovery

Bad Person
Am I such a bad person?
God knows how I try . . .
To be fair and honest,
Loving and open.
Yet I never find my way out.
Out of the guilt,
Out of feeling and being bad.

I wish I could understand.
I wish I could help others understand.

"But she was fine until now"

The true extent of the trauma, and often severe manifestations of serious mental health difficulties resulting from child sexual abuse, may not become apparent until five, ten, twenty or more years after the abuse. When this does become apparent so long after the abuse, many friends, family and lovers may experience confusion about what is happening to their loved one. The survivor may become immersed in major depression, unable to function in her daily routine. She may experience severe and constant anxiety and days and nights haunted by flashbacks and nightmares. Friends, family and loved ones have often been heard to say, "But she was fine until now. This can't have anything to do with her abuse as a child. That was so long ago." These statements reflect how little many of us have known about the long-term effects of child sexual abuse until relatively recently.

Were these adult survivors fine before their symptoms suddenly appeared? Clinical evidence points to the contrary. This section will introduce a small sampling of the dysfunctions common to adult child sexual abuse survivors to illustrate that everything has *not* been fine since the abuse. The damage incurred as a child has assumed many forms that have accompanied the victim through life, and many of them have gone unnoticed. Even if you were keen enough to notice dysfunctions or disorders in the one you love, you may not have made the connection between current difficulties and the sexual abuse of childhood. Adding to the difficulty of identifying this type of dysfunctional behavior as connected to child sexual abuse, many of the behaviors themselves may seem "normal" within our modern culture and therefore go ignored. The insight of a helping professional may be needed to see the interrelationships between the abuse of the past and current dysfunctional behavior. It will serve no purpose for you or your loved one if upon reading this section, you feel pangs of guilt because you didn't recognize the behavior as dysfunctional. The important thing is that if help is needed—get it.

We live in a society obsessed with thinness. Books, television and magazines all advertise the latest diets and exercise programs; all with the promise of being happy if we are thin. Yet eating disorders of all kinds are pervasively more common among sexual abuse survivors than among the population not reporting abuse in their medical histories.

Many child sexual abuse victims possess an obsession with their bodies in a way that, due to cultural norms at this time, may go unnoticed indefinitely. These individuals, primarily women, engage in a continuous cycle of dieting and obsessive exercise to control the shape of their bodies. The key words here are "continuous" and "obsessive" in differentiating this disordered behavior from a lifestyle that includes healthy eating and exercise.

This obsession may be carried to further extremes that *will* be noticed. A person diagnosed with anorexia nervosa becomes so obsessed with her body size that, no matter how thin she becomes, with her distorted self-image, she always sees fat and fat is the enemy to be conquered. To accomplish this goal, the anorexic engages in severe dieting or self-starvation, a pattern that often goes unnoticed until her weight loss is extremely severe and her very life is threatened.

Bulimics are equally as obsessed as anorexics with body size, but they are characterized as people who binge on food and then purge themselves, commonly by induced vomiting and/or ingestion of laxatives. These episodes of bingeing and purging serve to prevent weight gain.

On the other hand, the excessive overeater appears obsessed with food without giving a thought to body size, but that is not the case deep within herself. In relation to child sexual abuse, all three eating disorders manifest underlying issues that are the outgrowth of victims' traumatic sexual experience and the attitudes the victims adopt as a means of self-protection.

All three eating disorders often speak to victims' common need to feel bodily safe. There is often the internal belief that in being extremely thin or fat they can be safe from ever being the object of attraction of a potential abuser again. In addition, the survivor gains a sense of control over her body. As a child victim she was robbed of that control. Now, as an adult, she attempts to reclaim that power by controlling her body size through disordered eating habits.

The bulemic's bingeing and purging or the anorexic's self-starvation may be seen as an attempt by the survivor to attain the body of a young boy; one without curves. She may be in complete denial of her own sexuality, a sexuality repugnant to her because of its inner association with her first sexual experience as a young child. To be an adult woman with the body of a young boy is to feel safe from sexual encounters which terrify her.

The compulsive overeater is often attempting to put a barrier of fat between herself and possible abusers.

Child sexual abuse survivors are frequently body-shy. "Body-shy" is a term used to describe survivors' characteristic lack of ease, grace and comfort in their bodies. Take notice of the survivor's tendency to remain physically tense and rigid, qualities that reveal the survivor's lack of comfort with her body. Survivors frequently slump in a guarded posture and circulation may be suppressed, causing them to be easily chilled and for their skin to feel cold. It is not rare to find survivors generally clumsy and lacking in physical agility. Many avoid exercise and do not experience any pleasure in movement. They may dislike dancing, active sports and any strenuous physical activity. In addition, many survivors resort to wearing excessive clothing, inappropriate for weather conditions, or clothing several sizes too large for them. This clothing is often an attempt to conceal their body and feel a sense of protection from visibility and unwanted touch.

Child sexual abuse survivors are often very high achievers and perfectionistic in their endeavors. On the surface both appear to be desirable qualities but for the abuse survivor, both may be manifestations of her low self-esteem and her attempts to conceal this feeling. Striving high and doing everything to perfection are unconscious attempts to disprove the inner voice that continuously tells her how bad and worthless she is. At first glance these methods may seem an appropriate course of action to rid the self of its sense of badness by replacing it with positive outcomes, but two problems present themselves that illustrate how dysfunctional such a system is. First, the sense of inner badness is extremely strong and resilient and a great many positive accomplishments may only serve to weaken it. With only one error, one perceived shortcoming, all of the work done previously to get rid of "the bad self" can be erased. The second reason these attempts fail to eradicate "the bad self" is that they concentrate on "things" accomplished and only those accomplished to perfection. As with all people, the sexual abuse survivor's sense of self cannot be formed solely on "things." These activities and accomplishments provide some of the raw material we all use to formulate our identity but they constitute only one part of who we are.

A recovering abuse survivor spoke very wisely when she said, "For years and years I worked so hard to do everything perfectly, hoping it would erase how bad I knew I was inside. Then I realized I was Karen, the one who could do just about everything really well and it still wasn't enough—I still felt bad, like I was defective. I realized I wanted to be Karen the person, not Karen the person who did 'things.'"

Achieving near perfection brings the focus of others on the survivor's accomplishments and the survivor feels safe from having anyone focus on *her* too closely. The survivor's ultimate fear is that someone will see her inner "badness," know her horrible secret and reject her.

The qualities of overachieving and perfectionism become like a flashing sign carried by sexual abuse survivors pleading "Please like me," but it is a sign that adds "For what I do." Carrying the dangerous secret of their abuse, they are convinced that should their terrible secret ever become known, no one would look at them, like them and most certainly not love them. With this powerful inner belief, they set out to earn the love and respect of others by doing everything very well. The survivor believes unconsciously that having people like and respect her for what she "does" insures that no one will get too close and therefore her secret will remain safe. In a society that values excellence, many people marvel and admire what the survivor is able to accomplish without considering what is motivating such a driving force toward perfection. For many survivors this praise given by others for "things" they do, rather than who they are, serves as positive reinforcement to continue the perfectionistic behavior.

Child sexual abuse survivors may be prone to use addictive substances. With survivors striving diligently to feel good, it should not come as a surprise that a wide range of addictive behaviors are found in survivors of child sexual abuse. Through the use of addictive substances, emotional feelings can be temporarily numbed, preventing current or past pain from coming to the surface. Sadly, addictive substances not only numb feelings of pain but often numb pleasant sensations as well. Sandra spoke the sad truth of her addictive behaviors, "I didn't care if the nice feelings were gone along with the pain. All I knew was that the pain was unbearable, and I'd do anything and give up anything for it to stop."

If you observe the use of addictive substances by the survivor, professional help is indicated.

Untold numbers of child sexual abuse survivors suffer from a range of sexual dysfunctions as adults. These may range from total abstinence from sex due to feelings of disgust with anything sexual to sexual promiscuity. In recovery, many survivors often report they have not experienced sexual desires, fantasies, orgasm or successful sexual encounters at any point during their lives. They may report these disfunctions with a sense of profound sadness at the loss of a natural and beautiful part of what it is to be a human being. Spouses of abuse survivors may be unaware of the sexual dysfunction in many cases because the victim has too much shame to communicate that there even is a problem. Most survivors believe, yet again, that if a problem exists, there must be something wrong with them. As children, victims believed they were at fault for the abuse, now as adults, they believe any sexual dysfunction is also their fault.

Sexual abstinence seems like a logical reaction to the pain of sexual abuse, but you may ask "Why would someone so badly abused as a child turn to sexual promiscuity?" To understand why, it is important to view the situation through the eyes of the child who loved and trusted the adult who subsequently sexually abused her. Sometimes the abuser may constantly tell the child that he loves her and this is why he is doing this to her. Then again, he may threaten the child with loss of love if the abuse is discovered. He may threaten her with the idea that, not only would he not love her any more, but no one would. The threat that no one would love her is frightening. The idea that love can only be associated with sex can become internalized, and the child may come to associate any sexual act with being loved. As an adult survivor, still striving to receive the love she feels she missed as a child, this internalization may be re-enacted through promiscuity. Since, in childhood, self-worth was associated with sexuality in relationship to the abuser, it is not surprising that many survivors experience periods of sexually compulsive behavior. The idea that the survivor could be loved intrinsically for herself rather than what she has to offer sexually often seems like a foreign concept.

In other cases, abusers may continually verbally assault their young victims by calling them "whores" and "sluts" or other derogatory names even while abusing them. As untrue and as outrageously unfair as this name calling is when seen from an objective perspective, the child is not objective, and name calling can become a self-fulfilling prophecy.

The descriptions of disordered or maladjusted behaviors of adult survivors of child sexual abuse could continue and fill pages. The point is, during the time of the child sexual abuse experience to the present crises of beginning the long process toward healing, your loved one was not fine, even though appearances may have suggested otherwise. Many of the common dysfunctions go unnoticed or are often explained away as unimportant, the result of other forces in life. It is usually not long after the crisis of admitting the child sexual abuse, that friends, family, lovers and professionals are able to look back in retrospect and see that signs, subtle and not so subtle, had existed previously and could have suggested their loved one was experiencing serious difficulty.

While some of these behaviors were at one time highly functional ways to survive extreme circumstances, they no longer serve the survivor in a healthy way. The survivor's task is to translate these dysfunctional behaviors into behaviors that are healthier. You can remind the survivor to ask some simple questions to assist her with this difficult task of translating such as:

- Why is this behavior the best behavior you can come up with at the moment?
- Are there any better ideas that are healthier for the present circumstances?

Why remember now: traumatic amnesia

The trauma of child sexual abuse has an overwhelming impact upon the entire life of the young child. It is an experience which is outside the realm of normal human experience and an experience that affects every aspect of the victim's life at the time it occurs and later as an adult. The pain can be of such intensity that for the child who must endure the abuse and live within the system where it is occurring, survival becomes the ability to block from active memory what is happening. This is called "traumatic amnesia" and it occurs in a small number of child sexual abuse victims.

While constituting a complex psychological process, the abuse experience sets up a strong associative belief within the victim which simply stated is: To remember the abuse means to experience the unbearable pain and to experience the pain is to experience psychological death. The circularity of "to remember equals inextricable pain equals death" is thwarted by traumatic amnesia—the forgetting, blocking out of those events that threaten the very life of the victim. Simply put, to survive, to live, requires the extradition of the painful memories of what happened to the underdeveloped child.

Through the power of the mind serving to protect the survival of the individual, memories are figuratively transferred from a location where they are readily assessable, like the memories each of us have of our name, favorite color or what we did last Saturday, to a location that is inaccessible unless impacted upon by a powerful source. The inaccessibility of these memories is complete and may last for years or may even last an entire lifetime. It is an automatic process of survival. This traumatic amnesia can be understood as the unconscious attempt to defend against reexperiencing the victimization through memories.

This concept frequently causes substantial difficulty for victims' friends, family and lovers when memories do begin to surface. The question is often heard, "Why, if the abuse happened twenty years ago, is it just now coming out into the open?" The assumption exists that a person should have conscious knowledge that something as terrible as child sexual abuse happened and would have said something about it sooner. The pivotal word is is "should." The victim *has* had knowledge of what happened but traumatic amnesia had successfully blocked access to this knowledge in the past. She has not spoken out sooner because she could not. To say the victim does not *want* to remember is, in part, true because of the established causal circularity of the belief that to remember means loss of survival—death. The inner unconscious belief is so powerful that to remember and survive is seen by the survivor as impossible. But now something has caused these memories to be accessible, some event, some trauma has broken the lock the victim had on these memories.

To remember what happened later in life is to re-experience the inextricable pain that she believed was too intense to coexist with when she was a child. Yet, the reason these memories are coming up and have to come up is that repressing these memories results in inner suffering that won't go away. Remembering now is a chance to work through the abuse and its effects.

The hold that traumatic amnesia has over the painful memories of the sexually abusive past breaks when something is powerful enough to penetrate to the depth of these memories and rupture the protective sheath that surrounds them. It is common for survivors to begin to experience these memories in the form of recurring nightmares, intrusive memories and flashbacks of the abuse. It is important to be aware that intrusive and very vivid reexperiencing of the abuse during a flashback or nightmare, as if it were actually happening, is a natural response to a stimulus relating directly or indirectly to the original abuse trauma.

This stimulus could be a sexual assault, a rape, or being in a relationship that begins to become abusive. These are indeed powerful events that can break through the victim's inner core of protected memories because they are forms of re-enactment of the abuse endured as a child. The victim is taken back in time to the childhood sexual abuse. She may often begin to reexperience her sexual abuse; to feel the same terror, worthlessness and pain and begin to intensely remember what was forced upon her as a child.

Traumatic events can release the memories, however some triggers are often far less obvious or insidious. As human beings, we are endowed with a central nervous system capable of extreme sensitivity to sensory stimuli, as if the body had a memory of its own. These sensory stimuli can be as powerful in breaking traumatic amnesia as more obvious events. A particular sight, a sound, a visual image, or a taste experienced at a specific time, all can trigger the start of the powerful release of traumatic memories. The child sexual abuse, frozen in time, becomes alive and real again with all of its devastation. The death of the abuser, the birthday of the survivor's own child who has attained the age when the survivor was abused, hearing the story of another's child sexual abuse often triggers remembering one's own abuse. Sometimes, memories of the abuse rise to the surface for no apparent reason.

> *Cheryl and her family grew up outside of a metropolitan area on the family farm where they cultivated crops and raised cattle. When Cheryl and her husband got married they moved into the city where they both enjoyed successful careers, a good marriage and three delightful boys. When the oldest, Chad, turned seven he wanted to have his birthday party in Grandpa's old barn. Cheryl called her mother and they made all of the arrangements for the barn party.*
>
> *The appointed day arrived and the entire family, plus five friends of Chad's, headed for the farm. Cheryl's mother had put up decorations and brightly colored tables in the barn.*
>
> *Everything was perfect. Then Cheryl saw the shabby blue and white horse blanket, the one that used to be so vividly colored. She began to feel very nauseous but didn't know why. Suddenly she knew she had to get out of the barn. She felt tremendous fear and a deep pain within her. Her head began to fill with racing images of running around that barn. But it*

wasn't a fun race. She began to shake violently and gag. She saw herself as a child on that vivid horse blanket, when she had lost the foot race—with her father on top of her—hurting her. He had also insisted anything that went on in the barn was part of their "secret" game.

Cheryl had returned to her home many times before this party and had even been in the barn on occasion, but this time the horse blanket was in plain view and the sight of it was so powerful it ruptured a hole in the dam that held back her repressed traumatic memories, memories successfully secured from conscious awareness by her traumatic amnesia until that moment. Once the dam was breached it could not be repaired. The painful memories of the abuse she suffered at the hands of her father could no longer be contained and Cheryl began the long, painful process of reexperiencing that part of her past as though it had been frozen in time for all of these years.

It is not possible to avoid sensory triggers nor is it desirable to make such attempts. One of the goals of the healing process is to defuse the triggers by gradually reducing the severity of the reaction by learning new responses. When the survivor is experiencing a flashback or nightmare, you can help by providing reassurance like: "It's in the past." "You can handle it; you're an adult now." "The memory is no worse than what you've already been through and you've survived." "What are you able to do for yourself now that you weren't able to do before?"

When the traumatic period has passed you can help the survivor process and interpret the experience. Helpful questions include: "What was the trigger?" "What were you afraid of?" "Is there something going on in your life right now that reminds you of how you felt during the abuse?"

If the survivor is able to identify the stimulus that triggered the memory, she is likely to feel more secure and learn new coping strategies for understanding and preparing for future stimuli that may remind her of her abuse.

There is no one right way that survivors will remember their abuse. For some, like Cheryl, one image triggers an almost explosive series of vivid memories that pour out quickly, one right after another. For others, the process of remembering is much slower. Small segments of memories may emerge and take some time before they are finished enough to form one complete memory, and then the slow process begins again. Each survivor is unique and needs the time and space to remember at a pace right for her. It hampers the healing process if the survivor is pressured to hurry up and remember because she does not have control over the speed of her recollection.

The most important elements for you to know when trying to help a traumatic amnesia survivor are the following:

- **Traumatic amnesia is real.** It is not a deliberate attempt to deceive anyone by selective forgetting. It is an unconscious mechanism activated by the child victim and maintained by the adult victim in order to survive.
- **There is an underlying unconscious belief.** This belief is that to remember, to be conscious, is to experience a pain so unbearable that death will result. Thus to be conscious equals pain while to be unconscious equals survival.
- **The traumatic memories protected deep within the core of the victim contain the truth.** Held so deeply and closely, these memories have been out of the reach of the victim. They cannot be colored by attitudes of the present while they remain beyond awareness, so when they surface, what you see and hear is the absolute, unadulterated truth.

For all of these reasons, the memories of the adult child sexual abuse victim as they begin to pour forth speak only the truth. In committing to help heal the wounds of child sexual abuse, you also commit yourself to the survivor as you know her, and also to the personal truths of the abuse that occurred.

To disbelieve or to accuse the victim of lying at this time is to deny the very existence of the person and to reaffirm the basic belief that to have these memories—to be conscious and to remember—is inextricably linked with having to endure unbearable pain and death.

The healing process

Healing as a process, not an event. Its nature is not like that of a mild physical illness where a few trips to the doctor, some bed rest and possibly some medication can cure the problem. The wounds of child sexual abuse run extremely deep and require time to surface freely—

to be experienced as pain, loss and anger. The wounded need to know the truth and to work through the trauma that accompanies this awareness to attain true healing.

Ellen Bass and Laura Davis in their book, *The Courage to Heal*, outline six major stages in the long and painful process of healing.
1. Remembering
2. Believing it happened
3. Breaking the silence
4. Accepting that it wasn't your fault
5. Grieving
6. Anger

It is important to emphasize that these stages are not linear in nature. Stage three does not necessarily follow stage two, and the progression through stages five and six does not necessarily signal that the healing is complete. An appropriate analogy often used for understanding how these stages function in the reality of recovery is an image of a spiral. The victim often goes through the same stages repeatedly, each time with a different perspective and from a different level of healing. This progression through the different stages continues until the survivor no longer has a need to return to a particular stage in the spiral. At this point, healing and resolution has been attained.

To further clarify the healing process as a spiral rather than a linear process, consider the survivor who begins by having vague memories of being abused (stage one). The survivor may progress through believing and breaking the silence and then return to stage one as she remembers certain details of the abuse. Again she progresses forward but may skip believing it wasn't her fault and begin the grieving process for her lost innocence. Anger may follow grief and lead to more memories which take the survivor back to stage one. In time, the survivor will work through all six stages in the order and progression right for her.

The synopsis of the healing process is included at this point for several reasons. First, it provides a road map of the stages you will be likely to encounter in trying to assist someone who was sexually abused as a child and is now experiencing serious distress as an adult survivor. Secondly, it can serve as a quick reference guide as your loved one shifts focus along the spiral and can assist *both* of you in understanding what is happening and why and what actions you may want to consider at each point. This section also provides you with an overview of many of the particular elements of healing that will be discussed in more detail later.

This process of healing is a time-consuming one. It may take months or years to complete the full process. As the friend, family member, or lover, you should be aware of this commitment and be ready to respect the time and space it takes to heal. Years of pain and quiet suffering will not magically go away once the survivor has told her secret and experienced some of the pain. You may see her go through a complete cycle of the six steps and experience a period of relative calm only to have another memory arise out of a nightmare or flashback. Or a certain situation may trigger the emotions all over again in a slightly different way. It is important to remember that each time the survivor cycles through the six stages, she is progressing in the healing process. Remind her of this and remind yourself as well.

How can you help someone in the process of healing?

When a person tells you about being sexually abused as a child, that person is entrusting you with a part of his/her life that was and continues to be very personal and extremely painful. When entrusted with this long kept secret, supporters often think that they have to *do* something to help their loved one get over the pain. In reality, experiencing much of the pain is an inevitable part of the survivor's healing process which involves feeling the pain, grieving the losses and experiencing and redirecting the anger. The phrase, "You can't get over the pain until you face it and go through it," is well known among survivors who have been through the healing process.

Your role is not to make it feel better or less painful. You can't do that no matter how hard you try or how good your intentions are. Your role is to be a loving, empathetic supporter. You may also be able to give the survivor a very special gift that may be totally new—the experience of a healthy interpersonal relationship.

What the survivor needs most is someone who will listen, believe and give her room to experience all of the feelings that arise while she struggles to heal herself. The healing comes from within the survivor with the support of those around her. As a child, the victim's survival depended upon concealing his/her vulnerability. Now, as an adult survivor, the child within is still present, very frightened and often filled with guilt and shame, still very vulnerable, and in need of the help she didn't receive as a child.

The following are guidelines to help you support and aid in the healing process of your loved one.

The six stages of healing
Stage 1: Remembering

While traumatic amnesia and the later remembering are very dramatic manifestations of child sexual abuse, most victims know and remember their abuse, but they also know they may have consciously kept the secret of the abuse for some of the same reasons as the traumatic amnesia victim has unconsciously. They may have tortured memories that have haunted them all their lives and they may have repressed or denied feelings. Suffused with guilt, they are usually convinced the abuse was their fault. They may have used coping behaviors that are no longer appropriate. They may find that the abuse has distorted their responses to their own sexual feelings. They may be in relationships that are suffering because of responses that have been distorted by the child sexual abuse. Their remembering may not be as dramatic as a traumatic amnesiac's, but they too may be reexperiencing the child sexual abuse in response to events that are happening to them as an adult.

For those survivors that have always remembered their experience, healing may involve therapy that helps them to deal with their memories in a new, healthier manner, placing the anger and blame where it belongs, on the perpetrator. Ridding themselves of guilt can restore self-esteem and normal feelings to survivors. Their pain is no less than that of victims who have just "discovered" their abuse. It is just that they have been living with it longer.

For some others who haven't had access to their memories, remembering may begin slowly with vague feelings that they were abused, which they often try unsuccessfully to deny. In still others, memories appear as terrifying nightmares or flashbacks of vivid detail, often accompanied by a reexperiencing of the actual physical pain and terror of the original abuse. Memories of the abuse as well as the emotional and physical pain experienced at the time of the abuse, which were frozen in time as a means of survival, are freed and they pour out. Female survivors may experience vaginal and breast pain; male survivors may experience a squeezing pain in the penis or anus, both males and females may feel the sensation of gagging. The physical pain in combination with the emotional trauma make the remembering stage extremely difficult.

What you can do. Early in this stage there may be nothing you can do to help your loved one because the memories she is having are so frightening. Strong feelings of self-doubt about the validity of the memories may cause the survivor to feel that she is not yet able to share them with anyone. After stage three—breaking the silence—has begun and new memories arise and are shared with you, the best you can do is to listen empathically and believe what you are being told. Reassure the survivor that you are there and will be there to help in whatever way you can.

Stage 2: Believing it happened

Some survivors doubt their own perceptions of what happened to them when they initially start to remember the abuse. This disbelief serves as a form of protection against the loss of the belief about who they are, and what their family and life are and mean to them. These are powerful forces that conflict with tremendous energy against all that they are remembering about their sexual abuse. They may say to themselves or to another, "My father (brother, whomever) wouldn't have done this to me; I must be crazy." Such statements are reflective of the value placed on a desperate hope to hold onto an ideal that never existed except within their minds.

This self-doubt by the survivor may be very difficult for you. Friends and family members have said, "If she doesn't believe she was abused, maybe she wasn't." Keep in mind that to accept these memories as real means the survivor must let go the illusion of reality she has struggled to maintain. If the survivor accepts the reality of being sexually abused by a family member, what does that mean about her family? If abused by a member of the clergy, what is the meaning to be found in her religious beliefs? Many survivors need a period of doubt to ease into the realization that the abuse did occur. This is a period necessary for them to develop their own sense of truth and meaning about the experience. As a supporter, you can encourage the survivor to hang onto her doubt as long as necessary. With time, she will come to terms with the reality of her memories. The most important thing you can do is to believe what the survivor entrusts to you.

What can you do? Again, you may not know of the denial being experienced at this time. If you do, you can assist the survivor who is having self-doubts to believe what happened by filling in gaps you may be aware of and validate that what she is remembering *did* happen. These memories that bring with them unbearable pain and hopelessness are not the material of an over active imagination; they are very real and need to be seen as such. For other survivors, validate them, comfort them and believe them.

Stage 3: Breaking the silence

The survivor is now ready to tell someone about her abuse. She has carried the powerful burden of keeping the secret for years, sometimes even from herself, out of shame, guilt and because of threats made by the abuser never to tell anyone. Breaking the silence and telling at least one person can be the the most powerful stage in the healing process. And this process continues over time as more and more memories surface.

What you can do. Encourage the survivor to get professional help. This is the most significant advice you can give her. Yet, in the early stages of her breaking the silence, you may be the only person she can talk to. It cannot be emphasized enough that what is needed most by the survivor is a safe environment to assist her recall and then her work through the traumatic memories of her sexual abuse. To create this type of safe environment, listen, believe and validate what the survivor confides in you.

Survivors need to be heard and believed, even as they often doubt their own perceptions about the abuse. This self-doubt is not an indication that survivors are making up the story of abuse but is rather part of the process of coming to terms with the abuse. Admitting to themselves that their childhood was not a happy one, that their father or other significant figure was not a good person means the end—death—of an illusion to be mourned like any other major loss in life. Let the survivor know that you are available to listen to anything that she wants to share and that it will be believed and not questioned. The survivor needs your complete loyalty. Don't attempt to question the validity of what she is saying or ask for more details. That may result in her feeling disbelieved. *Never* sympathize with the abuser in any way. If you know this person, no matter how loving this person may have been toward you, the abuser did not have the right to sexually abuse another and does not deserve your sympathy.

Talking is a large part of the healing process. Sit with your loved one and let her talk on and on at her own pace. You don't have to feel the need to carry on a conversation. What she needs is to be believed and to release the burdensome secret and all of the feelings it carries with it.

In later cycles, breaking the silence may include telling other family members, friends and, even, a confrontation with the perpetrator. Helping the survivor at these times includes providing support of her decision to tell a wider circle of people. Continue to validate the survivor and her memories. Offer to accompany her on trips where disclosure will take place and be available when she is completed to help her process what happened and reinforce her that her actions are truly those of a survivor—not a victim. Confronting the perpetrator is more complex and deserves more space than can be allotted here, so a separate section, "Confrontation," has been included later in this book.

Stage 4: Accepting that it wasn't your fault

Child sexual abuse victims commonly believe that they were somehow responsible not only for the sexual abuse itself, but for actually causing it to happen. In addition, survivors commonly believe they should have been able to prevent the abuse or have been able to tell someone about it at the time. They feel guilty and ashamed for their perceived actions or inactions. It is not just the fear that they caused this awful event to occur, but also a belief that they *could* have or *should* have prevented or stopped the abuse that continues to burden them as adult survivors. It is common for survivors to hold a deep belief that they are truly a bad person to have had this happen to them.

What you can do. The survivor needs help in working to place the blame squarely where it belongs—on the abuser. Exploring with the survivor why she feels at fault will generally unveil some very strong distorted thinking such as, "I should have fought harder." "If

I had only been quiet when he came home from work this wouldn't have happened."

These examples provide clear pictures of the distortions that continue to hold the victim at fault for the abuse. They also provide the very tools you can use to dispute such thinking and to move the victim slowly in the direction of obtaining a clear understanding that the victim is never at fault.

Help the survivor understand why she couldn't say no effectively. Help her to see that her expectations are unrealistic for a small child. How would a six-year old have been able to fight harder against a grown male? Does being a bit too noisy mean that the perpetrator has the right to sexually abuse a child? Who was available to the child that she could trust to tell her secret and be believed and receive the help she needed?

Overcoming these distorted perceptions does not happen immediately, but your emphatically and repeatedly helping the survivor to see these distortions will help the survivor begin to place the blame on the abuser and not on herself.

Guilt and shame contribute to the survivor's sense that the abuse was her fault in another way. One of the most difficult and shame—producing aspects reported by survivors is the realization that they had experienced sexual arousal, pleasure or even orgasm during the sexual abuse. Such a realization fills them with tremendous shame and reinforces their sense of guilt. It may catch you off guard to hear that the survivor experienced sexual arousal during the abuse. It is important to remember that our physiological bodies respond to stimulation of the central nervous system and this response is automatic. It is not within our control as children or as adults. This automatic response is natural and is not a reason for guilt or shame. Explain to the survivor that this is a common, natural physical response over which she had no control. It does not in any way indicate she was experiencing emotional pleasure while being abused. Make it clear that this does not mean she wanted to be abused or that she was at fault in any way.

Stage 5: Grieving

The abused child, now an adult, has suffered many losses that have never been felt and grieved in order to reach resolution. His/her emotions were typically numbed at the point of the abuse, blocking the grieving process. This blocking also causes present repression of normal emotions. Repressed feelings become toxic over time if they are not expressed, and they can poison the system to such an extent that normal, healthy emotions, like joy and pleasure, have no room in which to reside and therefore cannot be experienced.

What you can do. Encourage your loved one to recognize the loss she has had in her life as a direct result of her sexual abuse as a child—loss of innocence, trust, personal integrity and esteem, friends, sense of family, perhaps even religion. Once the losses can be identified they can be experienced and mourned. This is a painful but necessary process for freeing the adult victim to become an adult survivor. Losses may well extend beyond those of childhood.

Loss of trust early in life affects subsequent interpersonal relations. There may be failed intimate relationships, on-going lack of friendships, an inability to maintain steady employment. One possible major loss, frequently recognized late in healing, is the loss of a dream, the dream of a life that includes normal loving relationships, children, a family of one's own. Recognizing these significant and painful losses touches off the grieving process and helps the survivor to keep the focus of blame on the abuser who must be seen as the cause for these deep feelings of loss. (See the section on Grieving and Mourning.)

Stage 6: Anger

For many survivors, their anger is self-directed. Just as they feel guilty about the abuse or causing the abuse, they may feel angry at themselves for allowing or causing the abuse, for failing to prevent it, or for not telling someone what was happening. Just as with their guilt, they fail to recognize that they were small, vulnerable children at the time of the sexual abuse. Some survivors have self-destructive feelings manifested in drug or alcohol use, eating disorders, or even suicide attempts. As with the assignment of blame, the survivor needs encouragement and support to re-learn to direct her anger squarely at the abuser and those who did not protect her as a child rather than at herself.

What you can do. Again, remind the survivor how vulnerable and trusting she was as a child and how being vulnerable and trusting is exactly how a child is supposed to be. She didn't do anything wrong. She was not a miniature adult capable of impacting on the actions of an abusive adult. Survivors need to remember and be reminded of this each time they begin to feel their anger being directed toward themselves. This does not mean advocating for physical aggression directed toward the perpetrator or others. No one advocates that anyone involved in child sexual abuse should be bodily harmed in anyway. The victim, least of all, should not be further harmed when her anger is turned inward, as in depression, self-destructive behaviors and suicide. Redirecting anger means finding an appropriate means of expressing the angry feelings.

You can help the survivor find ways to express anger. Encourage physical activity—pillow punching, stomping, throwing things, yelling, even breaking things in a safe environment. Provide opportunities for angry drawing, writing angry letters to the perpetrator—even if she cannot or will not mail them. These are all ways others have used to disarm their anger in healthy ways. Another verbal method is going to a deserted place and screaming everything she wishes she could say to her abuser.

The survivor may be unable to see these alternatives or may feel uncomfortable engaging in them alone. As a friend, family member or lover, make suggestions and offer to engage in the activity with the survivor. In this way, you provide support for the activity and you're available to provide comfort and support directly afterward when an outpouring of grief may follow.

Anger can be a primary emotion or a mask for other primary emotions that cause the feelings of anger to arise. As a mask, anger can bind us up in knots and render us unable to move, but its release can also free us from ourselves and open the way to positive change. (See the separate section on Anger.)

As a primary emotion, the expression and release of the built-up anger can leave the survivor feeling exhausted but also cleansed. The survivor has expressed her true feelings at long, long last.

Beating on pillows, screaming, drawing or writing should not be expected to resolve all of the pent-up anger a survivor has built up over time. It can be one important release of energy that is otherwise blocking the healing process. Frequently after a venting of this uncensored anger, the survivor is left with the primary feelings of fear, guilt and shame that have precipitated her anger. Letting the anger pour out enables the survivor to become more able to deal directly with these underlying feelings.

Remembering the past

As some survivors begin to remember and/or relive their traumatic past, they are embarking on a lengthy process that has no formal completion date, though there may be milestones along the way to measure successes achieved. One of the wonders of human nature is the uniqueness possessed by each and everyone of us. No two people are exactly the same and no two survivors will recollect or deal with their trauma at the same pace. If one woman has reconstructed her past in six months and is able to move onto the next stage, another woman may still struggle painfully after one year. Length of time is of no importance. Every survivor will and must move at a pace that is right for her survival. It has been said that we will only be given what we can handle at a certain time.

I stress the nature of our uniqueness here for two reasons. The first is to raise your awareness to the recognition that, for some, remembering the trauma of child sexual abuse is a process, not an event. It is like a continuum where memories seem to pour forth without any breaks at all and then dramatically slow or stop for a period of time. Your loved one can not be compared to another survivor who has moved past remembering onto resolution in three months. She does share having been victimized by child sexual abuse, but there the comparison must end. Differences in perpetrators, the intensity and duration of the abuse, the form the abuse took, the attitude and interpretation each child attached to the abuse, what has transpired since and what is happening now, all influence remembering, working out problems and healing. The point is that to help an adult child sexual abuse survivor requires that you truly see that person as being a unique individual, set apart from the other survivors in all ways. To make comparisons between the progress of one another is to deny this individuality.

The second reason for this emphasis is that the survivor is likely to engage in such harsh comparisons and self-defeating judgments herself. She may be thinking, "Why am I not doing better, so-and-so is." "I must be worthless. I must be truly crazy. I can't even do this right." This is very dangerous thinking that can lead to an array of self-destructive behaviors, the worst of which is suicide. To interrupt the progression from negative talk to self-destructive behavior, your commitment to help the survivor must include a commitment to individuality, a commitment to the unique way and speed which each survivor completes the process of remembering and dealing with memories, a commitment that your loved one is valued for who *she* is, with the abuse and its recollection constituting only one part of that person for whom you feel love and concern.

With this commitment fully embraced, you are prepared to
- Help the survivor recognize that he/she is unique—be specific.
- Reassure her that the process takes time and everyone needs to proceed at his/her own pace.
- Reassure the survivor that you are there for her and that you will continue to be there, however long it takes.
- Applaud each new memory breakthrough as a sign of true progress. Reassure the survivor that although the process is very painful and seems interminably slow, she truly is moving toward resolution.

An inability to make a total commitment to the individuality of the abuse survivor not only diminishes your effectiveness as a supporter, it also heightens the possibility of intensifying the negative attitudes and beliefs the victim holds toward herself. It is important to remember that these are people who, as children, suffered the trauma of sexual abuse, coped with the trauma by internalizing the idea that they themselves were bad, and this perceived badness replaced the reason they were being abused. This internalization of badness has never left them but has festered and grown.

When memories of the abuse start to surface, survivors often experience a heightened sensitivity to all comments and events that can be perceived as messages confirming their thinking of "I am a bad person." Awareness of this sensitivity will help you communicate without misinterpretations that may result in the survivor's stronger sense of inner badness.

The following examples may best illustrate this point.

What you may say	How it may be perceived
"Mary was abused but she is fine after 6 months of therapy."	"I'm a failure at this too. I should be better by now."
"Why is it taking you so long to get better?"	"I'm not trying hard enough. I'll never be any good."
"This whole mess is hard on the family too."	"I'm bad. I'm guilty because the family is upset now."
"Just pick yourself up and try and go back to work."	"No one hears me. I'm not worth listening to."
"I know this is hard on you but couldn't you stop crying for a while."	"My feelings are not OK. I need to get rid of them. I should just be dead."
"Remember, we all have problems too."	"I'm selfish for feeling this way."

As you read through these examples you may think they are exaggerations intended to make a point, but they are not. Each of these examples was contributed by a survivor and/or her support person. Communication when the survivor is so vulnerable should avoid reinforcing the negative self-assessment of the survivor during this fragile time.

Helping when the traumatic-amnesia survivor is remembering

Recalling the memories, feelings and meanings of the sexual abuse is an integral part of resolution but one which should not be over emphasized. Remembering feelings and meanings and remembering actual events and details are two separate and distinct factors that should not be confused. It is not necessary for the survivor to remember each incident of abuse to move forward. Some memories may simply be too painful to remember. Remembering that she *was* abused and recalling *some* of the specific memories of the time is enough. This stage of recollection is very painful and exhaustive and need not be made more difficult for the survivor by pressures to remember everything that happened to her as a young child.

One way you can can help your loved one is to listen, believe and validate her memories without exerting added pressure for more details.

You can help your loved one in other important ways when the survivor is remembering. When you are with her and she senses that a memory is coming, remind her not to fight it. These long repressed memories need to rise to the surface. It is in the best interest of the survivor to relax and allow the memories to come. As a memory surfaces, some survivors may get extremely frightened and their behavior may appear full of terror. A survivor may curl up in a corner or hold intensely onto a pillow and rock back and forth. These reactions reflect that the memory is not merely being recollected but is also being reexperienced in the present with all of its emotions, images and thoughts. Repeatedly reassure the survivor that this is "just" a memory, no matter how real it may feel to her. It is a memory and it will pass. Let her know that no one is there now to hurt her in any way. Let her know that you are with her and will protect her from harm. Even if, as a child, she didn't have anyone to protect her, she has you right now.

Once the memory has passed in its intensity, the survivor can be expected to experience some reaction to what has occurred. She may be completely exhausted, very tearful, angry or anxious. It will take a bit of time for her to recover fully and it is best to encourage her to take this time before doing anything else right away. Suggest lying or sitting quietly, taking a warm bath or engaging in some relaxation technique. What she has just experienced is draining both physically and emotionally and some quiet time is best to help her regain her composure. Let your loved one decide what is best for her.

Sharing these memories is an important part of the healing process. As a child, the survivor had to suffer alone. Thankfully with you there now, she doesn't have to suffer alone again. Let her know you are with her and willing to listen when she is ready, and encourage her to share her memories with you. As she does, remember to listen, support and validate her experience, both as a child and now as an adult survivor.

As painful as remembering is, it takes the survivor one step closer to resolution. One released memory is one less roadblock standing between her and her return to a healthy normal life. Help the survivor to view her painful memories as a step toward a time free from emotional, all-consuming pain. This is not an easy task, but with repetition, the survivor may begin to see growth toward healing.

The protective devices of denial, repression and dissociation all require tremendous amounts of energy to maintain even when they are executed at an unconscious level. When the memory has risen to the surface and been expressed, the energy once used for defense mechanisms can be put to healthier use. Explain to your loved one how much stronger she truly is for having survived another memory. Remind her that once the memories have exhausted themselves, all of her energy can be directed toward healing.

Encourage the child sexual abuse survivor to get help

Stage three in the healing process, breaking the silence, is most beneficial to the survivor when it includes telling his/her story to a helping professional. The qualified professional is best able to help the survivor through this part of the healing process. You cannot be expected to do it alone. The professional has the knowledge and resources that are necessary to handle the various stages of healing in a safe and effective manner and, as necessary, professionals may be able to prescribe medications to ease the survivor's path and to keep the adult survivor safe. Making this move to seek out and reveal her secret to a stranger may be extremely difficult for the survivor. Her lack of trust, overwhelming fear and enormous sense of shame and guilt erect imposing barriers to seeking out professional help.

You can help ease the way for the survivor to obtain professional help. Offer to help her locate a professional she can feel comfortable with. The survivor's family physician or a sexual assault center in your area can help you get started by making recommendations of capable professionals that work in the area of sexual abuse. Get several recommendations for a mental health professional. This may entail making telephone calls to various professionals or accompanying the survivor for support on initial interview visits. Remember that the survivor feels very vulnerable. She may not feel capable of asking the questions that need be asked to help insure selection of a professional who is both capable, and equally important, one with whom the survivor feels some level of trust.

Some questions you may want the survivor to consider include
- What are the therapist's qualifications?
- Has he/she worked with sexual abuse survivors in the past?
- What is the cost of therapy and how long are the appointments?
- Does the therapist have time available to see the survivor on a regular basis?
- Is the therapist available by phone in periods of crisis when the survivor feels intensely in need of help?
- Does the therapist favor group work and if so, does his/her office offer such a group or are they able to make referrals to one?
- What are the therapist's thoughts about hospitalizations and the use of medications?

After an initial visit with one or more therapists, the survivor may need help processing all of the information she has received and help in making the selection of the professional that would best serve her needs, although the decision must ultimately be her's. You can help her process the information she has received without attempting to make the decision for her. Discuss the key questions above with the survivor after the initial interview and then further discuss
- How did she feel about what she heard?
- Did she feel more uncomfortable or comfortable with a given therapist? (This recognizes that the first visit is seldom very comfortable for anyone.)
- Did she feel any reservations about working with someone of the therapists gender? Some women prefer to work only with women, while others prefer to work with men. Either way, what is important is that the survivor be at ease with the gender of the therapist and believe she can trust in him/her.

This can be a very scary time for the survivor. Let her know that you are there to help and support her in whatever manner she would like. Help her to schedule her first appointment if she would like you to. It may be helpful to offer to accompany her for the first few appointments. She may feel more comfortable beginning her therapy with you along as support. Discuss with the survivor what you can do and then leave the decision totally up to her. In this way, you offer support and provide the survivor the opportunity to feel empowered by making her own decisions.

Unfortunately, the adage "buyer beware" is applicable to therapy as well as other areas of life. Many, many professionals are fully qualified and will be a wonderful support in the survivor's healing. But there are also professionals in the field who can cause further harm even though they claim expertise or are known to work with survivors of child sexual abuse. Help the survivor remain aware of her feelings while working with the professional she chooses. If she begins to feel discomfort or further victimization in therapy, it is time to confront the therapist, terminate the therapeutic relationship, if necessary, and get a new therapist.

Within our culture we tend to put complete faith in medical professionals. Some of these people may have unresolved problems and unmet needs of their own and they may attempt to resolve them with their clients. This is never OK. The therapist-survivor relationship is a very unique relationship. It is common for the survivor to admire, depend on and feel attracted to her therapist. When the therapist accepts or encourages these feelings in a sexual or romantic way, the process of therapy has been thwarted and becomes destructive to the survivor.

Warning signs

The Task Force on Sexual Exploitation by Counselors and Therapists points out that there may be clues to a lack of professionalism or misuse of power by therapists such as
- The therapist avoids or refuses to discuss the survivor's feeling that something is wrong during therapy.
- The survivor has the feeling that therapy involves giving in personally to the therapist rather than therapy as a learning process.

- The therapist suggests any mutual activity that is uncomfortable to the survivor.
- The therapist exhibits unprofessional behavior which feels sexual such as
  ○ Telling dirty jokes
  ○ Undressing during therapy
  ○ Eying the client up and down
  ○ Discussing the therapist's sex life.
- The therapist exhibits unprofessional behavior that gives the survivor "special" status by
  ○ Making out-of-the-office appointment or scheduling appointments for after normal officehours
  ○ Making secrecy a part of the therapeutic relationship
  ○ Using the survivor for personal support.

If your loved one becomes concerned about what she is experiencing in therapy, let her know that you believe her concerns and encourage her to trust her feelings. The therapeutic relationship is a mutual contract that may be terminated by the survivor or therapist at any time. This is important to remember. If the survivor is feeling uncomfortable, exploited or victimized by the therapist for any reason she has every right and obligation to herself to discuss her discomfort with the therapist. If resolution cannot be arrived at, she should terminate the therapeutic relationship and seek out a professional who can meet her needs.

Group therapy

An alternative or supplement to individual therapy for the survivor is group therapy facilitated by a skilled professional. For many survivors, the idea of one-to-one therapy is overwhelming or they may find the need to augment their therapy with a group of others who have felt what they are feeling. In both instances the value of group therapy can be very important.

For some survivors, it may be too difficult to place their trust in an individual professional until they regain some of their ability to trust anyone. Group therapy can provide an opportunity for this growth by

- Bringing together people who share a common bond. All participants have experienced the pain of abuse and are

affected by its aftermath.
- Providing members with the knowledge that they are not alone and here they can get the non-judgmental support of the other members who know what they are experiencing.
- Providing the time needed to begin to trust and speak of the survivor's own issues at her own pace. The survivor is not immediately thrust into a face-to-face situation with someone who needs her to open up to in order to begin the process of healing.

Many mental health centers offer special group therapy for sexual abuse survivors. Friends, physicians, crisis centers and your local mental health association can all serve as places for referrals to groups available in a given area.

This discussion of groups is not meant to tell the survivor or her supporters that going into a group will be easy. It is never easy to begin to tell others of the terrible secret the survivor has been carrying. It is best to give the group a trial run, at least three to four sessions, before deciding whether or not the survivor feels comfortable enough to remain in the group. If the survivor is feeling uncomfortable, encourage her to speak to the facilitator who may be able to help her overcome her discomfort with that particular group or perhaps suggest another group that may be better suited for the survivor's needs.

Groups are also being developed around the country to support the friends, family and lovers of child sexual abuse survivors in their attempts to help their loved ones through the healing process. These groups offer the same benefits as therapy groups offer to the survivors and can be very beneficial as you progress through this long, often painful process of helping another heal the deep wounds of child sexual abuse.

Communication

> *When Kim broke the silence of her abuse and became seriously depressed, it was like a veil of silence fell over her world. Friends and family politely spoke to her in conversations that had no substance. Others failed to keep in contact*

at all. If she tried to talk about what was happening to her or how she was feeling, the conversation seemed to change automatically to some other topic. For a very long time she wondered what was wrong with her. She felt depressed, scared and very much alone.

Finally, in one of those benign conversations with her mother she asked, "Why don't you talk to me, really talk to me?" The answer she received shocked and saddened her. Her mother, and others, were afraid to truly talk to her, afraid that if they should say the "wrong" thing, Kim would become more depressed and possibly take her own life. The solution Kim's family and friends chose was to say nothing meaningful at all.

This erroneous thinking is more dangerous to the well-being of the survivor than talking about what is happening. When breaking the silence and telling others her horrible secret, the survivor's worst fear is that she will be disbelieved and rejected by those she has chosen to trust with this hidden part of herself.

When disclosure is met with silence rather than validation and concern, the survivor is left to misinterpret the lack of response. Against the backdrop of her inner sense of badness, her interpretation frequently confirms her inner thoughts; that she is bad, unlovable and uncared for. This is very distorted thinking, but with a lack of information obtained through conversation with those close to her, such conclusions are common among survivors. Remaining quiet may also send a message to the survivor that, once again, her feelings don't count. The survivor is no different from others who try to communicate with someone and meet a blank stare or quick change of the topic. Survivors wonder what is wrong and their vulnerable situation leads them to believe that what is wrong is them.

When friends, family and lovers are too frightened to approach the subject of the abuse and the survivor's current struggle, there is a often a message that the survivor is still a victim. The message conveys that the survivor is too weak and vulnerable to emotionally handle speaking about the abuse. Reinforcing the victim role encourages the sexually abused to remain stuck in that role rather than continuing to take the risks involved to progress to the role of survivor.

The refusal to talk openly with the survivor is often an expression of fear. "If I say the wrong thing you will kill yourself." This sets up a power differential that further strengthens the role of a helpless victim. It says, "I am more powerful than you and I can control your actions." The victim knows very well what it is to be in a relationship where power is used to control them. This hierarchy of power is constructed more by what is not said than by what is actually spoken. Consider what is not said. "I won't talk about the abuse to the victim because my words are so powerful. If my words are so powerful, then I too am powerful; and since the victim couldn't handle the power of my words, the victim is unempowered." This mirrors a relationship not unlike the abusive one, a relationship where the individual with the power (abuser) entices the powerless (victim) to trust him because he "knows what is best" for her.

While the adult survivor may currently appear before you in the grip of crisis, it took tremendous bravery and power to finally break the silence and begin to tell her story. These are not the actions of a weak, powerless person.

Keeping communication open expresses your love and concern for the adult survivor. It is a reminder that she is valued; that her life has worth; and that you see her as a person of power and strength who will survive and thrive. If what you have to say to your loved one contains messages that invalidate her story of the abuse or conveys disbelief in what she is saying to you, then it is best that you be honest with her and let her know that you don't feel able to give her what she needs at the present time. Your honesty will be valued far more than a silence left to interpretation.

To accentuate the danger that exists in a lack of communication with the adult survivor, consider the following scenarios where you are the party in distress and have just confided in a close friend or relative about the nature of your emotional turmoil.

> **Scenario 1**: Your confidante arrives to visit and inquires how you are doing. As you reply, "Not very well," he/she asks if you want to talk about it. Given the indication that your friend is genuinely concerned, you begin to speak and very

soon you have a dialogue with your friend contributing support, validation, asking questions for clarification and adding a new perspective for your consideration.

Scenario 2: Your confidante arrives and asks how you are doing. As you reply, "Not very well," he/she agrees it's been a terrible day and proceeds to give you all of the details. You interject that you'd really like to talk about how you've been feeling but your friend says, "You don't want to do that, it will only make you feel worse."

In the first scenario true communication is occurring as a dialogue between both parties. Questions express genuine concern, listening expresses the value placed on the other individual, and validation says, "I believe you." With this form of open communication, even if painful topics arise, they are unlikely to precipitate suicidal ideas which stem from a sense of worthlessness and hopelessness.

If the communication resembles that in the second scenario, the friend goes out of the way to divert conversation away from the troubled areas by talking about him/herself. The survivor's concerns are ignored, invalidated and she is told both what to think and feel. Out of this scenario the typical elements of suicidal ideas, worthlessness and hopelessness are more likely to arise.

If the concern exists that communication will worsen the current condition of the adult survivor and may lead to suicide, the opposite would appear true. To be ignored, invalidated and unsupported increases the sense of being a victim—powerless, hopeless and worthless. These are the dangerous components of suicide. This is not to ignore the possibility that the survivor is feeling suicidal before you arrive and, as she speaks about her pain, those ideas may become stronger. Even if this is the case, communication is the key. If you are talking and listening to the survivor and talk of suicide arises or you suspect the survivor may be considering it, communication provides you with the information you need to intervene and prevent a suicide attempt. (See Suicide Prevention/Intervention.) Communication is the largest part of the healing process. If you are going to make the commitment to help the survivor to heal, you also make the commitment to open communication.

The following guidelines can help you in your communicating with an adult survivor.
- Communicate as you would with any other close friend/relative.
- Be genuine and empathetic.
- Listen to both her verbal and nonverbal communication. Be aware of both what she is saying as well as her tone, the manner in which she sits, the amount of eye contact she can maintain. Frequently survivors will look away, assume a fetal-like position or change facial expressions when they are not comfortable discussing something, even though their words may say, "Yes, I'd like to talk about that." Be aware when the verbal and nonverbal communication is not saying the same thing and talk to the survivor about what you are seeing and hearing. She may be unaware of the separate statements she is making, and your gently drawing attention to this contradiction may act to give the survivor the permission she is seeking to admit she is not yet ready to tread into a certain area.
- Be honest. Do not attempt to deceive the survivor.
- Ask questions to clarify points in a non-threatening manner. You may be tempted to ask, "Why didn't you tell anyone?" this may make the survivor feel she is again at fault, Rephrase your question to, "Could you say more about how you felt keeping the abuse a secret?" This is far less threatening and allows the survivor to open up and express how frightening a time this was and what it meant to have been abused.
- Respect the survivor's right to say no or to refuse to answer a question
- Ask how you can be of help now.
- Don't avoid sensitive subjects.
- Express your own pain as you experience it. You can serve as a wonderful model that acknowledges feelings are neither good or bad, they just are.

All of us have a need for interpersonal communication in our lives. Talk to the survivor so she can, in turn, talk back to you and share a part of herself too long kept a painful secret. There's no better way to verbally express your love and concern. The survivor can be empowered if you respect her right to decline to answer any question she does not feel comfortable answering. Remind her of this often. Communicating openly and honestly with the survivor aids in her healing by giving to her the gifts of empowerment, trust, respect and honesty.

Guilt

Self-blame is a major barrier to the healing process because as long as the survivor feels guilty for the abuse, she is not free to work completely on restoring her self-esteem and releasing pent-up anger. The self-blame frequently experienced focuses on the survivor's actions immediately preceding the abuse. "If I had been quieter." "If I had been a good girl." "If I hadn't made Daddy mad." In these common statements of survivors, the child victim assumes complete responsibility for the sexual abuse. These statements are never a valid cause for any sexual assault. No one ever has the right to abuse another, regardless of a prior action. It will help if you emphasize this repeatedly when self-blame arises as an issue. For the child victim, and later the adult survivor, these self-blaming statements foster guilt and ignore the vulnerability and complete dependency the child had on the abuser. The child is no match for an adult whose intent is to have sexual relations with him/her. Nothing she could have done before or during the abuse could have altered what happened to her.

Adult survivors are often intellectually able to see that thinking they were to blame for the abuse as a small child is distorted, but emotionally they are often unable to accept their inaction and inability to protect themselves. They have extreme difficulty accepting the total feeling of helplessness that they experienced as victims.

There appear to be a number of items that contribute to the amount of guilt experienced by survivors in the long-term.
- Being told directly or indirectly by the abuser that they were responsible for what happened.
- Being abused by someone they knew well.
- Being disbelieved or punished if they tried to tell someone what happened after the abuse.
- Not attempting to escape from the abuser.

- Survivors whose self-blaming tendency is reinforced by others who point out their mistakes and question their judgments.
- Survivors who are sensitive to others; feeling and striving for harmonious relationships.
- Survivors who have never told their secret. Silence leads to feelings of being the "only one," which enhances self-blame.

As you listen to your loved one speak of her "guilt," there are a number of things you can do to help her begin to heal herself in this area.

- **State unequivocally that she did not ask for nor did she deserve to be sexually abused.** No matter what the survivor did or did not do prior to the abuse, regardless of what she was wearing, no matter what she said, she did not deserve to be sexually abused.
- **Help the survivor see that her actions during the abuse constituted a choice for survival.** Whether the abuse occurred inside or outside of the family unit, a child is completely dependent upon the adults around her for survival. Submission to the abuser was a choice for survival.
- **Remind the survivor that she was a small, vulnerable child, no match for a mature adult.** Expectations which may be an appropriate response for an abuse situation as an adult are likely to be very inappropriate when applied to the world of a small child.
- **Remind the survivor to interpret her actions in the context of the terror that the small child was experiencing at the time of the abuse.** Looking back on any situation, it is easy to say what one should have done differently. Given the context of the time, the survivor did the very best possible.

What most survivors need is reassurance that their behavior is understandable and "normal," given the circumstances. They may need this reassurance repeatedly while they are healing. Helping to provide this reassurance can work to ease their guilt over not making the "best" response at the time because "best" can not be defined within the context of a small child.

Dissociation

"Dissociation" is a word that sounds ominous to survivor and family, friends and lover alike. The term often conjures up of all sorts of bizarre thoughts and images—a sort of Jeekyll and Hyde transformation of an individual. The first task is to dispel these horrible myths.

Dissociation is a natural human defense mechanism that we all possess and can use without conscious direction. It is used particularly when we are under very significant stress. Consider sitting in your office feeling overloaded at 10:00 a.m. The next thing you remember you are still sitting in your chair. You're still holding your pencil over an empty writing tablet and the time is 10:10 a.m. You have no recollection of your thoughts or feelings for that ten minutes and the blank tablet is evidence that you haven't been working. What has happened here is that you've dissociated from yourself as a means of dissipating the stress you were experiencing. Dissociation is a type of time-out to allow the central nervous system to slow itself down and manage stress.

It is the also the turning off of a survivor's sensory responses.

If you begin by thinking about dissociation in this way, it will be less ominous and more understandable to view the dissociation experienced by many adult child sexual abuse survivors who have unconsciously honed this skill to perfection. The quintessential word here is "unconsciously" and more will be discussed on that in this section.

For some survivors the defense mechanism of dissociation is widely experienced and developed far beyond the capabilities of adults who have not been abused. This development is in direct correlation with the abuse and the instinctual need to survive the ordeal. The child who is sexually abused is neither physically or psychologically ready for such an experience. There is the physical pain of sexual relations between a small, underdeveloped child and a mature, fully developed adult. Frequently there is also the pain of some kind of physical restraint and sometimes sadistic rituals whose sole purpose is to inflict pain on the victim for the sexual satisfaction of the adult. Psychologically there is immense pain experienced when an adult, unequivocally trusted by the child, betrays that trust. Adults know how painful it is to feel that their trust in another has been betrayed. This painful experience is magnified untold times for the child victim because in a large number of the instances of child sexual abuse the betrayer is the parent, the one person in whom the child has complete trust and dependency to meet her basic needs. Since the survivor was prevented from physically leaving the abusive situation, the only remaining option is mental escape.

Additional psychological pain is experienced when children blame themselves for what happened and also for somehow directly causing the abusive events to take place or failing to prevent it. Both the physical and psychological pain culminate in unbearable pain and the very survival of the child depends on dissipating this build up of the trauma.

It is here, as the child is being subjected to the traumatic abuse, that dissociation happens. To withstand, to survive the occasions when Daddy or any other abuse perpetrator begins the act of sexual abuse, the child dissociates. She seems to split off from herself so she is separated from her physical self or is physically and psychologically turned off to sensory stimuli. She is temporarily free from the experience despite its continuance.

Once begun, dissociation quickly becomes automatic and is easily activated by minimal environmental or psychological cues. Dissociation continues into adulthood and is particularly accelerated as previously repressed memories of the abuse rise to the surface with all of the pain and trauma experienced as a small child. A common dissociative state during these times is to experience the world as flat, much like a television set that the survivor is watching but not participating in. Such sensations often convince the survivor, and may cause you to speculate, that she is truly going crazy. Dissociation usually does not mean that the survivor is psychotic or has a split personality. Both are extreme diagnosis which are comparatively rare among survivors, as is the occurrence of multiple personality disorder. It is helpful to remind this type of survivor that she is not crazy at all but that she dissociates when the current stresses become too painful.

There are many forms of dissociation.
- Periodic drift outs or daydreams
- Fugue states and amnesia where a period of time is blocked from memory

- Multiple personality where some life experience is split off as a separate entity from the whole person
- Denial and repression of the abuse

For purposes of this book, it is important to realize that dissociation is a form of self-protection learned initially by the child to survive the inescapable pain of the abuse. It is helpful to empathize with the survivor's fear of loosing time or feeling like a spectator to the world, but it is helpful to be firm that neither of these frightening sensations is a sign of insanity. Without new coping strategies to take its place, dissociation continues to protect the survivor from the terrible pain as she recollects her abuse. As new coping strategies are developed in therapy and practiced by the survivor, she can be assured that dissociation will become less and less frequent because it will no longer be necessary for self-protection.

The survivor's ability to dissociate can impair her ability to form much needed emotional bonds with others because the survivor may appear unfeeling, distant and cold. It is unfortunate that a survivor is most likely to become "numb" as a spontaneous defense when strong emotions are present—the time when she is likely to appear "unfeeling" to others. As a supporter, try and remember that the survivor is shutting down in the context of victimization as a learned response which originated when she tried to escape the trauma during the abuse. Unfortunately, over time, this reaction has become automatic and generalized to other anxiety-provoking experiences. You can help the survivor by supporting her efforts to assess and name the cause of her anxiety once a dissociative episode is over. Assessing and naming the source of the anxiety is a technique which provides the survivor with a strengthened awareness and responsiveness to the present.

It is appropriate to return to the statement made earlier, that dissociation is an unconscious defense mechanism. Neither the child who is being abused nor the adult survivor recalling the trauma makes a conscious decision to split off from him/herself when the pain, the fear, the anger becomes too painful. It is not an active, conscious avoidance of the situation—it is an unconscious mechanism that is activated for the purpose of enabling the victim to survive.

Believing that the dissociation is a deliberate, conscious attempt to escape reality can have disastrous effects on your efforts to help.

If you believe this is deliberate, your response is likely to be harsh and judgmental and judgmental comments once again tell survivors they are deliberately running away rather than facing up to reality and getting well.

As a friend, family member or lover you may never even notice the short times your loved one dissociates. The body becomes very still and the eyes tend to glaze over much like a common blank stare. As the episode ends, there may a slight jerk of the body, like that experienced when you are startled, and the individual returns to whatever she was engaged in before the episode began. It appears much like an ordinary daydream. Since to disassociate is to split off from oneself, from conscious awareness, the person has no knowledge that anything has occurred during these intervals.

Longer periods of disassociation, constituting hours or days, can be frightening for you and the survivor. During these episodes, the emotional stress may be building for days or weeks and the victim often experiences a sense that "something" is growing within her, something she cannot name. As one woman told everyone close to her, she felt like there was a bulb in her stomach growing bigger and bigger each day and that she was afraid she would explode. The "explosion," to use her terminology, began on Friday and did not end until Sunday afternoon and was an extended period of dissociation.

Friday she kept her regular appointments, then returned home extremely upset after an incident at the gas station. That is the last conscious memory she had until Sunday afternoon when she found herself on the floor of her room surrounded by pages of paper she had scribbled on and two bed pillows slashed with a kitchen paring knife.

She was frantic and terrified over the lost time and certain that she was now completely crazy. With the help of her therapist she reconstructed the reason for the dissociation.

For weeks Katie had been talking about anger that was surfacing seemingly out of control and without sufficient cause. Anger is one of the emotions that has consistently caused Katie a great deal of anxiety because she feared she would loose control and, rather than expressing it as it arose, she suppressed it.

On Friday she had become angry with her therapist and, in the style she is accustomed to, she said nothing—she suppressed her anger. She could not have known at the time that her system could not handle one more piece of suppressed anger and, since healthy expression was blocked by her fear and anxiety, the only avenue of expression was for her to dissociate from herself and let that part of her scribble angry notes and slash pillows. In this way the anger was not really hers, at least while she was dissociated.

The slashed pillows may raise questions of safety when someone dissociates in this way. To ease some of the fears you may have, Katie took her anger out on inanimate objects because of her inability to express her anger at the person involved. Had this been possible, there would have been no knives or pillows necessary to release these built-up emotions. When dissociated, the survivor is very rarely a risk to anyone else. The risks involved are those of the anger she has toward herself, and all safety precautions should be taken.

Isolation

Isolation can be the worst enemy in the healing process and yet many survivors repeatedly tell of the profound sense of isolation they experience once the secret of their past abuse has been revealed. This feeling of estrangement may be the result of several elements: their primary emotions of shame and guilt, distorted thinking, acute awareness of their overwhelming depression, childhood messages, and actual experiences of losing friends and others who have previously provided them with support. Regardless of the cause, survivors frequently feel completely alone, which can become a self-fulfilling prophecy. We all tend to act as we feel. If you believe you are alone, you become alone through your inadvertent actions, even when your strongest desire is for the support of someone else.

Powerful feelings lead easily to distorted thinking. The survivor may view herself as a "bad" individual responsible for her abuse and frequently feel that she doesn't deserve anything or anyone good in her life. She continues to hold onto the belief that she must keep her secret: That if people *really* knew about her, they would surely see her "badness" and reject her. As a result of this distorted thinking, survivors often protect themselves from their anticipated humiliation and rejection by separating themselves from others. Some survivors are certain that others can see that they were abused, like they wear some kind of sign that says, "I was abused," marking them for all to see—much like wearing the Scarlet Letter of days of old. This isolation only serves to increase their distorted thinking because it provides proof of their unworthiness to have friends. They may think, "I have no friends because I am a bad person," rather than thinking, "I have no friends because I believe I am a bad person and pull away from others so they will not know of my abuse. And I can then protect myself from their rejection of me."

In addition to guilt and shame, the deep depression experienced by many survivors often teams up with distorted thinking to increase their isolation. The survivor is all too well aware of her preoccupation with the abuse, her increased irritability, periods of uncontrolled tears, or the fear that she will loose control and begin to cry anywhere. This leads her to believe that she is not fun to be around and that friends, family and lovers don't want to spend time with someone who is not fun. The result is self-sacrifice. She gives up her need for support and isolates herself from others due to her faulty beliefs and thinking.

Many survivors grew up in dysfunctional homes which taught them very strong messages about feelings, control and independence that reinforce their isolation as adult survivors. If feelings of sadness and anger were not acceptable within the family as a child, this belief is frequently carried forward, and emotions become no more acceptable as an adult. If controlling displays of emotions was emphasized to children, outbursts of tears or anger over their abuse get personally labeled as "bad" by the survivor and need to be brought back under control. When this is not possible for a time, the only solution survivors may see is to isolate themselves from others to insure that no one will see their perceived weaknesses. If the family stressed independence as an honorable trait, the messages replayed as an adult survivor often include: "Don't bother others with your problems," or "You must be strong enough to take care of yourself." These thoughts, which seem completely illogical to adults, become increasingly logical to survivors who feel as vulnerable as when they were child victims.

Not all isolation experienced by the survivor is the result of her primary emotions, distorted thinking or childhood messages. Many survivors begin to experience actual isolation as friends, family or lovers back away from them due to a lack of understanding, fear or disbelief. As they watch their loved one struggle and emotionally crumble, it is not uncommon for family and friends to become confused and fearful. Lacking the understanding of what is happening and why, often the fear of doing or saying something "wrong" sets in and they begin to stay away and say nothing at all. Their own self-protection against these uncomfortable feelings may cause them to begin to pull away from the survivor. *This does not make them bad people.* Their intent is not to add further hurt to the survivor. They are people, whose instinct for self-preservation is activated to avoid those things that are frightening, confusing and unpleasant. As a result, however, the survivor experiences a stronger sense of isolation due to the actual losses of friends and families.

Regardless of its causes, isolation is devastating. Human beings have a need for others, a need to belong which is lost once isolation begins and accelerates. It is important to view isolation as a protective mechanism that once started, accelerates into more and more time alone.

How can you help?

Be available to the survivor. Learn all you can about child sexual abuse and its long term effects. Listen and accept the survivor as she is, from moment to moment without judgment, and validate what she is telling you. These are the first and primary steps toward helping end the cycle of isolation. It is very important for the survivor to know she has one person to turn to and be unconditionally accepted.

Involve the survivor in activities with you. This will help reinforce that you are there for her and are to be trusted. This is a difficult issue for many survivors to overcome. Keep your activities simple. Remember how vulnerable the survivor feels and allow her to work her way up to activities that involve a group of people.

Reassure the survivor that regardless of the rejection encountered by any others, you still love and believe in her and are empathetic to her pain. If the survivor is rejected by one person, she may begin to generalize this rejection, thinking that everyone will reject her. Your continued support serves as a reality check that not *all* people will react in the same manner. Your continued support can help break the cycle of distorted thinking and enable the survivor to take additional risks with new people.

As the survivor begins to widen her circle of experiences, offer to accompany her for a while as a support person. If you both go to the shopping mall and the survivor becomes very uncomfortable or begins to panic and wants to run out of the store, don't resist her need to do this at this time. Getting comfortable being with people will take time and practice, and it must be done at a pace the survivor can tolerate.

Support and acknowledge any efforts the survivor makes on her own to leave the safety of her home and venture out. Let her know that you view this as real progress and acknowledge how difficult it must be at first.

Encourage the survivor to talk to her therapist about becoming involved in a support group. Support groups share a common bond that helps members feel more comfortable than a group of people at a party. There is comfort in knowing that those sitting around you truly understand what you are feeling because they are or have experienced the same feelings in the past and can offer encouragement and suggestions based on their experiences.

Isolation can be fatal. The survivor who becomes cut off from social support is more subject to the overwhelming feelings of hopelessness that may lead him/her to attempt suicide to end the pain. Isolation can lead survivors to thinking that nobody cares, values them, or will miss them if they end their lives. Having your continued support keeps the survivor in contact with someone who will listen, validate her feelings, and help her view her distorted thinking for what it truly is: *distorted.* The survivor can then begin the task of working to overcome such thinking, knowing she can turn to you for support, validation and reality checks. Reality checks are when the survivor confides in you some thought she is having and asks whether she is thinking clearly and logically. Don't lie to her. She has taken a tremendous risk in asking the question and wants an honest answer from you.

As an example

The survivor says, "Even my best friend doesn't believe I was abused. Nobody will. I feel like I'm going crazy."

The support person says,"Not everyone will react to you in this way. I believe you and there are others who will believe you. You are not alone in this and you are not crazy."

Be patient. Overcoming old messages, fears, guilt, shame and distorted thinking will take time and practice. The survivor may need to ask you the for the same validation repeatedly until she can finally bring herself to believe in your response. Don't take this personally. It is a reflection of the lack of ability to trust that stems from the experience of the abuse and not from your relationship with the survivor. Trust betrayed at such a young age takes time to heal. With your support and encouragement it can heal.

Post Traumatic Stress Disorder and depression
Post Traumatic Stress Disorder

Many survivors of child sexual abuse benefit from being diagnosed as having Post Traumatic Stress Disorder (PTSD). PTSD refers to the psychological reactions that typically occur as a result of a disaster or other extreme psychological stress, such as war, airplane and automobile accidents, tornadoes, floods, earthquakes and physical and sexual assault.

A combination of the following criteria accompany PTSD.
- The existence of a "psychologically distressing event" that would evoke significant disturbance in almost anyone.
- Later reexperiencing of the trauma in one's mind through recurrent dreams or "flashbacks" (intrusive sensory memories) to the original traumatic situation.
- "Numbing of general responsiveness" to avoid the external world; for example, dissociation, withdrawal or loss of interest in daily events.

A wide variety of other symptoms are
- Extreme reaction to touch or to any reliving of the original abusive experience.
- Intense feelings of fear, terror and helplessness.
- Symptoms of major depression and anxiety.
- Panic attacks resulting from exposure to a situation or object that reminds the survivor of her abuse.
- Feeling detached from others, or the inability to feel emotions of any type, especially those associated with intimacy.
- Sleep disturbances, difficulty concentrating, memory problems and irrational guilt.

The essential element of this disorder is that the event that has occurred, for our purposes—child sexual abuse, is psychologically distressing, beyond the range of normal human experience and is an event that would be "markedly distressing to almost everyone."

The impairments of Post Traumatic Stress Disorder may range from mild to severe and affect the individual's entire life. Impairment often includes difficulty with interpersonal relationships, development of self-defeating behaviors, suicidal actions, or the use of alcohol or drugs in an attempt to further numb the pain associated with remembering the events, the very patterns we have found in sexual abuse survivors.

A PTSD diagnosis is helpful for many survivors of sexual abuse because it has a normalizing effect. When the symptoms being experienced by the survivor are explained as initially reasonable, and in many cases valuable, efforts to survive extreme psychological stress, the survivor begins to see herself reacting in an understandable way. This new insight can be helpful in overcoming the tendency to blame herself rather than the abuser. In addition, the explanation of PTSD by a professional provides the survivor with a valid way to understand her current difficulties rather than fearing that she is going "crazy."

Depression

Major depression is not uncommon to adult survivors. Research on adults molested as children report that depression is the most frequently reported symptom. Major depression is serious and requires serious action. Major depression is distinguished from the depressions each individual experiences from time to time by its duration of two weeks or more and the display of significant physical symptoms that can include constant fatigue, unexplained aches, changes in sleeping or eating habits, the inability to relax, slowed speech or body motions, slowness and confusion, an inability to make decisions, and suicidal thoughts. A person in a major depression can feel overwhelmingly hopeless and worthless. She may express destructive self-blame, shame, no longer caring and the absence of pleasure in anything.

The sense of hopelessness and powerlessness that accompanies major depression severely constricts the survivor because she can see no future beyond her current state of distress. Many survivors express this sense of hopelessness when asked how they would like to see their lives. Their response is frequently that they can't even imagine a time different from the present when the pain and horrible nightmares will pass. Without a positive sense of the future, the survivor is living in relationship to the abuse rather than meeting her needs in a healthy context.

Survivors, in their efforts to describe their indescribable depression, frequently speak about being at the bottom of a very black hole with no way of getting out. One woman described her major depression as a black hole but one with living hands and spindly fingers to reach up and pull her back down if she climbed too far toward the top.

The seriously depressed survivor should be closely monitored and her therapist notified immediately. If the survivor expresses self-destructive thinking or has a plan and method of suicide in mind, treat the situation as a crisis. (See Suicide: Do not ignore the signs)

The combination of on-going therapy, that can be intensified during these periods, and the availability of antidepressant medications can help reduce the symptoms of a major depression and keep the survivor safe. Listen closely to your loved one for any expression of depression or suicidal thoughts and do not hesitate to take action. A major depression is far too serious and potentially dangerous to delay action in the hope that it will pass on its own.

You can help by making yourself available as an empathetic person for the survivor to confide in. Encouraging and allowing survivors to put their feelings into words is a healing process that prevents the survivor from denying the reality of the problem. A nonjudgmental partner can provide an objective response or another perspective to the survivor. This is extremely helpful in assisting survivors see where their thinking may be going astray and focus on one problem at a time. You may be able to supply the survivor with hope and courage to rise out of her depression by sharing experiences that have provided you with strength and hope in the past.

Suicide: Do not ignore the signs

Depression is a frequent dark visitor to the adult survivor. With the depths of depression, thoughts, plans and attempts at suicide are all too real. The survivor feels absolutely powerless over her life at present and indescribibly hopelessness. She may begin to believe that her life will never get any better and to live it as it is would be unbearable. The only natural solution the survivor may be able to see is to take her own life because it promises relief from suffering and creates pseudo self-respect. Before you dismiss the idea of self-respect gained from suicide, consider what it would be like to feel absolutely powerless. You can't stop the crying and the shaking. You can't get up and go to work or school. The horrifying nightmares of your past plague your sleep leaving you exhausted and terrified. The feeling is that you're going completely crazy and can never recover. In contemplating her situation, the survivor sees suicide as a way to stop the pain and to regain power, to have some small control over her life by ending it.

When depression becomes hopelessness, death by suicide becomes a a serious risk. It is important that you understand the reclamation of the power component in suicide attempts of those who have been sexually abused if you are going to help your loved one.

How do you know if the one you love is contemplating suicide? While this may sound like a stupid question, it is not. Too frequently we believe we would have no difficulty recognizing someone who is suicidal, that suicidal people are overt in their actions. Maybe this is the result of seeing too many movie and TV dramas where a person is crying and screaming, "I'm going to kill myself," while holding the weapon to do it. While these scenes sometimes do happen in real life, they are far from representing the majority of suicidal situations.

Some warning signs of an impending suicide attempt published by the Suicide Prevention Taskforce include

- Depressed mood
- Changes in sleep and/or appetite patterns
- Increased social withdrawal
- Loss of interest and pleasure in activities previously enjoyed
- Preoccupation with themes of death
- Giving away important possessions
- Verbal expressions about self-death
- Use of alcohol or drugs
- History of previous suicide attempts
- History of any form of abuse

The best rule is: If you're going to err, do so on the side of safety. If you observe a cluster of the warning signs listed above, act on them. If your loved one confides in you a desire or plan to take her life, even if only subtly or in a joking manner, act on what you hear. Trust what you feel—your intuition. If you begin to suspect suicide is being considered, you're likely to feel fear, a sense of uneasiness, and mounting anxiety. Trust what you're feeling and act on those feelings.

How to act when you suspect suicide is being considered

There are a number of myths about suicide that may be deadly.

MYTH: Those who talk about suicide will not actually do it.
FACT: In almost every suicide, there is a steady effort by victims to express their fear and frustration and complete hopelessness. This communication is not always verbal but when notice is given, it should be taken very seriously.

MYTH: Asking someone, "Are you thinking of committing suicide?" may lead the survivor to attempt it.
FACT: Asking such a question may in fact lessen stress and lead to productive life-saving counseling. It interrupts survivors' thought processes that they are completely alone and clearly lets them know you are concerned about them and their safety.

MYTH: Only a mental health professional can prevent suicides.
FACT: Anyone who is concerned is often very effective at preventing suicide. If you are concerned, you can probably help.

There are no prescribed sequential steps to take to prevent a suicide in every situation with every individual. Each person is different. The following techniques and guidelines are provided to aid you in making the necessary decisions based on the specific situation and the resources available in your particular area.

Listen and affirm. The survivor in a emotional crisis needs someone who will listen and really hear what she is saying. Every effort should be made toward understanding the feelings that lie behind the words. If you're told how unbearable the pain is and that the only way to stop it is to die, affirm what she is saying by responding to what she is feeling. By saying,"I can see how much pain you are in and how difficult it is for you right now, but I want you to know that these feelings will not last forever," acknowledges your understanding of her reality. In contrast, if you respond with,"You don't want to die, you have so much to live for," you are ignoring the depth of her current despair and the understanding she is seeking is lost. If the argument, "You have so much to live for," is used, it must be an absolutely genuine and specific response that the survivor can relate to directly in this time of crisis. "The kids and I really love and need you." "You're very important to me as a friend (sister, wife)." Both may be honest expressions of why the individual may in fact want to live.

Affirm the anger being expressed by the survivor. "You're very angry because you were so deeply hurt by (name of perpetrator). You have every right to be angry and express your anger, but why should it be against yourself? You've already been hurt enough. You need to direct your anger squarely where it belongs—at the one who caused it."

Evaluate the seriousness of the person's thoughts and feelings. If the survivor has made clear, self-destructive plans, the crisis is very serious. Ask questions. Does the survivor have a plan or a timetable of her intent to take her own life? Does she have a method planned and implements nearby to complete the suicide?

When a plan exists, take immediate steps to get emergency assistance. A plan is an important indication that the survivor has given long and serious thought to suicide and is not acting purely on impulse.

The key element is whether the person has a specific plan and at what level of seriousness this plan is. While no talk of suicide should be ignored, the following continuum illustrates the seriousness of the intent and the need for immediate action. Even those at low risk for suicide require professional assistance and should not be ignored.

Assessing the risk. Assuming a survivor is already in therapy, the following would apply. If a survivor is not in therapy and you know he/she has any ideas of suicide, encourage him/her to begin therapy immediately.

1. **Low Risk:** The survivor discloses thoughts of suicide, often very casually, with a therapist or friend.
2. **Slight Risk:** The survivor discusses thoughts of suicide with a therapist or friend and develops a plan of action.
3. **Increased Risk:** The survivor is now openly developing a plan. Advise her therapist so medication amounts can be monitored and the therapist can explore the underlying issues that have arisen to produce the current crisis.
4. **High Risk:** The survivor has a plan and has a determined method This survivor is at high risk for suicide and immediate suicide intervention by a professional is necessary.
5. **Extreme Risk:** The survivor has gone to within one step of carrying out a suicide plan. He/she may have purchased a weapon, stockpiled significant quantities of medications or made other arrangements to implement the suicide. Immediate intervention with potential hospitalization is indicated to insure the individual's safety.

Take seriously every complaint and feeling the individual expresses. Don't dismiss or undervalue what the survivor is saying to you. In some instances, the survivor may express his/her difficulty in a very low-key manner but beneath this seeming calm may be hiding profoundly distressed feelings. A person who calmly states he/she wants to be dead should not be treated less seriously than one who is crying and screaming the same words. All suicidal talk should be taken seriously, if not literally.

Don't be afraid to ask if the survivor has thoughts of suicide. Survivors may make comments that express suicidal thoughts but not openly state their intent during a crisis period. Experience has shown that harm is rarely done by directly inquiring into these comments.

You may not get a direct answer; you may not get any answer; but any information you gain by making the inquiry can be extremely helpful in assessing the situation. Directly asking, "Are you thinking about suicide?" can open the floodgate of thoughts and feelings the survivor has been holding back. Knowing that someone is there and is concerned about him/her as a person whose life is valued can interrupt the very thought processes that have brought him/her to consider suicide.

> Diane was extremely depressed for days and had not spoken to anyone about the way she felt. She barely moved from the couch, feeling unable to move, unable to do anything and sleeping each day and night in her clothes. Her younger sister, Julie, lived 150 miles out of town and called one night, knowing of Diane's difficulties but not of the severe depression she had sunk into.
>
> After their telephone conversation, Julie immediately got in her car and drove 150 miles to see Diane. When she arrived and saw her sister in such a state on the couch in her rumpled clothes, she sat down and asked "Are you thinking about committing suicide?" Diane was shocked. The answer was yes but she didn't know how Julie could have possibly known this. Julie calmly responded "We have to talk about this," and talk they did for hours and hours. Julie called Diane's therapist. The two of them were able to help Diane see that this was not what she really wanted. What what she truly wanted was for the pain to stop and there were other ways to accomplish this.

There are times when you may ask this question and be met with overwhelming hostility from the survivor. He/she may lash out at you verbally or physically as if you are a terrible vicious enemy that must be slain. For some, you are the enemy. Asking the question poses a threat to their sense of pseudo power mentioned earlier; the power of last resort that suicide promises the survivor. If you're met with a hostile response, try and remain focused. The attack is not against you but against the perceived threat your words possess. Try not to take it personally. For the survivor to admit to suicidal thoughts and plans is to give up the last perceived vestige of power she believes she has over her life. It becomes critical, absolutely essential, for the survivor to try and maintain her power, to defend herself against someone she perceives as trying to take it away.

The intense feelings of being threatened now are frequently acted out in a manner you would expect from a very frightened child; it may be a reenactment of the abuse trauma, but this time the frightened child also feels anger and lashes out. She may scream, kick, try to throw things, and bang on the floor. If you can keep this frightened little child in mind, it will be easier for you to remain calm and to help your loved one calm herself. What you see before you is an adult and because of this you may expect adult behavior even in the time of crisis. You need to look closer to see the truly frightened child that doesn't yet know the adult ways of being heard, of getting her needs met, of not being abused. If you are unable to calm the survivor in this emotional state, call for help. Her therapist is the best first call and, if this is impossible or she has no therapist as yet, contact your local crisis intervention center. They will know how to handle the situation safely and effectively.

State your support. Let the survivor know that you're there for her right now, unconditionally. Tell her that you'll listen. Hold her if she desires to be held. Beat on pillows with her to release the anger. When some calming has taken place, the survivor often needs your support in another way. She needs to know that you'll continue to love and care for her even now that you know she has had real thoughts of suicide and possibly acted like a child having a tantrum.

Do not avoid seeking assistance. Don't try to handle everything alone. Call for help. This is as much for you as for the survivor. To help diffuse some of the perceived threat of outside help, clearly state your intentions to the survivor ahead of time, step by step. Let the survivor know that you're going to call the therapist or the local crisis invention line because *you* need help.

At all costs, don't try to dupe the survivor. Don't convince her that a ride in the night air will be helpful and then drive her to the nearest emergency room. This only adds to her feelings of being deceived once again. It diminishes rather than builds a sense of power and control, and it may seriously damage the relationship of trust you share. If you believe the hospital is a necessary next step, if the therapist or crisis center has advised it, state so directly. The reaction you receive may be intensely angry but in the long term the survivor will come to understand that you did not deceive her. The trust of your relationship, while shaken, can be rebuilt.

Ask the survivor to make a suicide agreement with you. This is a written contract that states the survivor will not attempt to kill herself or harm herself in anyway and that she will seek out help whenever she begins to feel this way. While it is impossible to stop people from killing themselves if they are determined to do so, this agreement can help sustain the survivor through a time of acute despair. The agreement is a concrete symbol that she is loved and of value to someone at a time when she feels completely unlovable and worthless.

Help the survivor create a safe place for these periods. Having the survivor stay with you or another supportive person during these crisis periods can help her to feel safe and cared for. In addition, a change of environment may break the crisis period because pictures, furniture or odors where the survivor lives may fuel the crisis with associations and memories.

Realize that the talk about suicide and the failed suicide attempts are a cry for help—a cry for someone to step in and intervene in a life that seems out of control. Exhausted by anger, pain and depression, the survivor feels unable to help herself and unable to ask someone for help. The threat of suicide or its attempt speaks in the loud voice she cannot seem to muster.

Understand that, very often, suicide is not about dying. If you believe that suicide is about death, it is not unlikely that after multiple unsuccessful suicide attempts you will grow angry and judgmental toward the survivor and withdraw your support. This withdrawal may send a powerful message that says, "If you're going to kill yourself, I wish you'd just get it over with." This is not an easy attitude to acknowledge but one that may grow if you do not understand that suicide is more about pain, anger and depression than death. If you can view the suicide attempts as a cry for help or an attempt to stop the pain, you will be more likely to feel empathetic and to remain in the relationship with the survivor. Hearing the cries for help, you can offer help: a genuinely loving ear to hear the pain, a shoulder to provide support when times get tough or to catch the tears shed in anger, grief or despair. It is a perspective that recognizes and honors our humanness; that both victim and significant other need and provide help to each other throughout life, especially in times of crisis. It is a perspective that recognizes that it's all right to need help, to ask for help and to receive it.

Self-mutilation

Some survivors of child sexual abuse engage in self-mutilation, and this behavior is a very serious sign that the person needs professional help.

To attempt to understand self-mutilation, it may be helpful to view it as the unnatural continuation of the pattern of harm from abuser-to-victim transferred to victim-to-self. Having experienced such pain as a child, the adult survivor may believe she deserves to suffer and begins a cycle of inflicting pain upon herself.

Self-mutilators may physically harm themselves by repeatedly cutting their bodies with knives or razor blades or burning themselves with cigarettes or hot stoves. As unusual as it may sound, the survivor often attains some temporary relief from the self-mutilating act. When the pain inside becomes so great as to be uncontainable, the survivor may cut herself to create a place where the pain can exit to the outside.

Self-mutilation may also be an attempt to experience feelings. A survivor who is emotionally numb yearns to feel like those she sees around her and to experience at least one of those feelings—physical pain. For example, during great emotional pain she may burn herself repeatedly with a cigarette.

Self-mutilation can also be an expression of forbidden anger from deep within, however irrational this may seem. If the survivor learned that anger was a "bad" or "evil" emotion as a child, she may be unable to express this emotion openly as an adult. She may turn to self-mutilation as an expression of her anger against her abuser.

Lastly, self-mutilation is often a distorted way of coping with memories of the abusive situation. By inflicting pain and abuse on herself, the survivor indicates she still believes she deserves this. She has learned to expect it; it is what is familiar to her.

It is important to understand the connection self-mutilation has to the abuse experience. This is not an area for amateurs, and professional help should be sought as soon as any self-mutilating behavior is observed. As a friend, family member or lover, you can discuss it with the survivor and continue to provide your support, but helping your loved one is best done by a professional who understands the complexities of this behavior and its relation to sexual abuse.

You might contact the Hartgrove Hospital Program for the Treatment of Self-injury. The hospital is located in Chicago. Call toll-free 1-800-DONT CUT. The number is not a hotline, but the staff can direct you to help in your area.

The Healing Journey

Understanding
I wish I could understand what happened.
    Nothing falls apart so quickly...
It fades ever so slowly,
    Eroding away the very base on which I stand.

Words fall like rain on a sand sculpture,
    Washing away a little sand with each drop,
Until there is nothing left of the sculpture.
    A thing of great, simplistic, pure beauty
Gone forever.

How can I rebuild this same sculpture?
    I can't.
I can never find the same grains of sand,
    The right mixture of moisture to hold it all together.
    If I manage to recreate a piece which resembles the first,
    I stand on guard day and night,
With the painful memories,
    And the fear of the coming rain.

From *victim* to *survivor*

There comes a point during the healing process when your loved one will make the transition from child sexual abuse *victim* to adult *survivor*. It is not a definitive point which can be predetermined or planned, but it is a point at which definite changes in the individual become apparent both to herself and to those around her. The feelings of absolute helplessness begin to give way to the recognition that she does indeed possess power; power over her own life in the here and now that was not lost in her traumatic past. It is a point where increased self-esteem begins to replace her personal beliefs of "badness" and "worthlessness."

Small things may signal this transition.
- The person's posture becomes more erect.
- Eye contact again becomes a part of her healthy communication.
- She shows new confidence in entering settings where people have already gathered.
- Periods of profound depression begin to decrease both in intensity and frequency, and suicidal thoughts cease.
- Social contacts increase, a sign of healthy risk-taking.
- If there has been an absence of sexual interest or lack of acknowledgment of her own sexuality, a healthy new interest in sex may now replace those feelings.

It is important to note that while these are welcomed, wonderful changes to be whole heartedly celebrated; they mark the ending of one process and the beginning of another. Your loved one need no longer be a *victim* of her child sexual abuse, but she will always be a *survivor* of it. The abuse remains as an important chapter in her life story. It cannot be erased through healing but it is now beginning to be put in the perspective of her entire life. As a survivor, the memories of abuse remain but without the substantial power they have held to directly affect subsequent chapters as her life story continues to be written daily.

As a victim, there was no future because the abuse consumed everything. As a survivor, not only is there a future, but that future begins to open to new possibilities as the abuse is placed within the context of her life; much like a single chapter in an autobiography. The chapter is there, it can be referred to, but it will never again have the power to dictate what else gets written into the book of the survivor's life story.

Until this time arrives, as friend, family member or lover, you can be very instrumental in facilitating growth in this direction by becoming aware of how you speak to your loved one.

Resist seeing this individual as a victim and let her know often she is a survivor. This requires diligence on your part. As you listen to and understand the pain of your loved one, you too can begin to experience some of that same pain and react to it. Try not to say things like, "You poor thing, this shouldn't have happened to you." "You were a just a sweet little girl." These statements may seem sympathetic but they reinforce feelings of victimization your loved one may be continuing to experience. Words like "poor thing," "happened to you," and "sweet child" exude victimization and strengthen the individual's conception of herself as a victim, both then and now. Your loved one is struggling to break free of a cycle of victimization that began with the abuse and has continued into the present time. Instead, reminding the survivor of the many ways you see her as a survivor will help break the cycle of victimization.

Replace sympathy with empathy. Empathy expresses your understanding of her pain; sympathy alludes that you feel sorry for her but does not denote understanding. Through empathetic listening, you can express your understanding of her pain and help her see that she is no longer a victim. She is not small and vulnerable anymore. She has survived that very difficult period of her life and is now a mature adult who has power over her own life, even though it may not always feel that way.

Point out the ways that you have observed her use of power. You might remind her of the times when she has asked for your help and made the decision to refuse attendance at functions where the abuser would be present; how she started to record her thoughts, feelings and progress in a journal; how she attended her support group regularly despite the times she really wanted to stay at home and how she made the decision to seek professional help or to call a crisis center when in need of emergency counseling. Even the decision to get out of bed and fix herself something to eat in the midst of the depth of depression is a sign of being a survivor and is one to be applauded loudly. These actions are those of a survivor, not a victim. It is helpful to remind the survivor of these actions frequently so she increasingly becomes better able to incorporate them into her view of herself as someone who is surviving.

One woman who was interviewed was continuing to struggle with her college courses despite a disabling depression. She transferred her course load to an independent study program to enable her to study at home and she taped a blank poster board to the bedroom door. Every time she received a grade slip, she posted it on this board. What she was erecting was an "I can do it" reminder board. Whenever the depression would get intense and she would feel completely hopeless, she would look at the board of college grade slips and know inside of herself that she could do it. She could survive because she was already doing it, and the grade slips were her proof. The same principle can be used for any number of accomplishments that serve as reminders to the abuse survivor that she is surviving.

Help increase the survivor's sense of self-esteem. In the midst of the healing process, it is common for the survivor to overlook her other accomplishments, strengths and self-awareness in areas having nothing directly to do with being an abuse survivor. It is common for the sexual abuse survivor to have extremely low self-esteem. It is not only that her abuse experience as a child was bad, but her internalization that what happened means that she is bad. To reduce, and eventually eliminate, this false sense of badness, work must be done to increase self-esteem.

Self-esteem can come from accomplishments and strengths accumulated throughout life. Especially important to survivors of sexual abuse, these accomplishments and strengths present an argument to the self the facts which support the role of survivor. Remind the survivor of her past accomplishments: in scholarship, art or music for example, and discuss how these successes indicate she is a survivor. Make a list of these accomplishments with the survivor so she can refer to it often and see the concrete evidence of a person who has worth and deserves to feel good about herself.

Jenny was 35 and the mother of three young children when she first started remembering her childhood sexual abuse. She became severely depressed and did not even have enough energy or desire to care for her own children. Jenny's husband, Dave, made arrangements for child care and became actively involved, helping Jenny through the professional therapy she had begun. Dave spoke about periods when Jenny's depression was overwhelming; of how she didn't wish to live because she was such a horrible person, and horrible people can't be good wives or mothers. Her depression told her that the only way to rid herself of this awful person she felt she was—and everyone else would soon know—was to take her own life.

> Dave contacted both her therapist, who wanted to see her right away, and a crisis intervention center. Dave explained to Jenny that they were going to the hospital to see her therapist. In the car he began to calmly talk to Jenny about all of the things she had done, the strengths she possessed, and how no one who is so horrible could possibly have done all those things. Jenny was resistant, saying all that was fine but that they were all things "before all of this."
>
> Dave countered, "Before all of what, the abuse? That's not true. The abuse happened when you were seven years old. These wonderful accomplishments occurred after the abuse, not before. You've been a wonderful wife to me and a loving and caring mother to our children, who love you completely. Would they love a horrible person? Everyone you work with likes you and has the deepest respect for your integrity. And volunteering to coordinate that major fund raiser was not the sign of a horrible person. These are the parts of you that make you special, lovable and admired. They can not be taken away now because you remember your pain as a child and how horrible that made you feel."
>
> Jenny was much calmer when they arrived at the hospital. Dave had reminded Jenny that she was a person of worth. The memory of abuse could not take that away from her. Through specific examples of her activities, efforts and accomplishments, Dave reminded Jenny that she was an adult of some stature now, not that small helpless child stuck in the attitude that she was worthless.

If we feel like a victim and view ourselves in that way, we will continue to be a victim in all areas of our lives because a victim feels no sense of power over life. For the abuse survivor, each rejection, no matter how small, is a reminder of how it felt to be sexually abused as a child.

Each trust that is betrayed holds the same devastating impact as the child betrayed by a parent or other perpetrator. The survivor in early recovery is walking a tightrope between these old familiar and painful feelings of continued victimization and new feelings of positive assessment. Reinforcement provides a shift in self-perception that restores power. The survivor may now say, "This is horribly painful but I know I will make it, I am making it and I will survive."

This reinforcement will not magically sink in in a single episode. The survivor needs to be reminded over and over of her worth. The abuse has caused a negative mindset over years of time. It will take more than one session of positive mental medicine to eradicate this mindset.

Your persistence in giving the survivor this gift of affirmation provides a major impetus toward helping her experience positive change and helping her to be able to move forward in the process from remembering pain (being a victim) to resolution (being a survivor).

Touch

Child sexual abuse survivors frequently experience extended periods of time where they are hypersensitive to being touched by other people, and this sensitivity may extend to friends, family members and lovers. This sensitivity (See PTSD and depression) manifests itself in a number of exaggerated startle responses, particularly when the survivor is touched in any way without prior notice. For some, the reaction may be to pull away suddenly, to dissolve into tears, and/or to strike out at the individual who has touched them.

> *Alice was taken to an emergency room for stitches for a severe cut she sustained at work. She didn't experience any difficulty as the doctor cleaned and stitched the wound. When the medical care was completed, however, Alice's hypersensitivity to touch manifested itself as the doctor attempted to comfort her by putting his arm around her shoulder. Alice began to sob uncontrollably and she physically attempted to strike the physician.*

This reaction was not the result of a conscious decision on the part of Alice to strike out at the doctor. It was an unconscious reaction occurring in a split second, a response to the early abuse when Alice was touched against her will. These kinds of responses are exaggerated startle responses.

When you're sitting outside enjoying a summer evening and a wasp is suddenly buzzing around you, you may flinch, duck or even jump up and run away, or you may be more aggressive and find something to kill the wasp. If you've been stung before, you don't want that to happen again. You don't think to yourself, "I think I should run or slap that wasp so it doesn't sting me." You just automatically react based on what you know of wasps and the memory of the pain of a wasp sting from past experience.

This reaction is not so different from Alice's reaction. She also struck out in fear based on her previous experience of older men touching her—her abuse as a child.

The touch of another, particularly if that touch is unexpected or perceived as sexual in nature, may trigger a signal of threat to a survivor's inner child, a child who was unable to protect herself against her abuser in the past. The reaction by the survivor is an exaggerated response of self-defense, a response that says, "No one will ever touch me again without my permission," and, "No one will ever abuse me again."

This hypersensitivity is commonly associated with touch that is perceived as a threat by the survivor. In Alice's case, no such threat existed as long as the physician's touch was restricted to the task of tending to her injury. In essence, she gave the physician permission to touch her in treating her wound, but when he touched her without her permission by putting his arm around her, she instinctively overreacted.

Sometimes victims may extend this hypersensitivity during periods of extreme trauma when they may be unable to tolerate even casual contact with others that can occur in a grocery store or shopping mall.

When and if your loved one begins to experience an extreme hypersensitivity response, she will typically feel very embarrassed by her actions. The first thing you can do to help her is to discuss the reasons she is having these reactions and reassure her that it is an uncomfortable part of her recovery, but one that will pass.

Secondly, help the survivor arrive at a short phrase or word she can say to herself if she begins to feel she is in a situation where she may feel threatened. Some examples include: "I'm safe." "Breathe!" "I am (name) here and now." "I'm not a small child." Said repeatedly, a mantra of this kind may serve to connect the survivor with the present and help calm her before she spontaneously reacts to the sensation of being touched.

When you have been very close to the survivor and your attempt to reach out to hold and comfort her during difficult times is met with her pulling away, screaming or crying harder, it can hurt. Try and remember
- This is not a rejection of you personally or your attempt to comfort her, but an unconscious response she may have used as a coping mechanism in the past.
- This is a startle response because the past and present have become blurred and the survivor again feels threatened.
- This is not consciously done. It is a conditioned response to a perceived threat.
- Extreme reactions such as this will subside with healing.

Most importantly, take extra care and caution in your touching of the survivor, particularly in times of acute distress. Instead of reaching to comfort her automatically, ask the survivor if she wants to be held or to receive a hug. This gives her control over when and by whom she is touched. Be deliberate in announcing your touching. Remember the past and present of the survivor may be very blurry to her. Announce your intentions and actions clearly, "(name), I'm going to hold your hand for a little while." While this may sound silly, it provides the survivor with the information she needs to remain connected with the present, and it provides a warning system to disarm her startle response.

As human beings, we all need to be physically touched by others throughout our life span and the adult child sexual abuse survivor is no different. During her healing process, however, she may have conflicting needs: one for nurturing and loving touch and the other for control over her body. With a little extra care and attention to her sensitivity, you can help her through this period. You can continue to provide loving touch to her by acting carefully and acknowledging her fears in the process. By doing this you are showing that small frightened child within the survivor that touch does not have to be scary and threatening, but it can be warm, loving and nurturing. You are in the process of rebuilding the trust of a child that was so badly damaged years ago. Be patient, go slowly and try not to take rejection of your touch personally. Time, patience and repetition will work to overcome this hypersensitivity to touch and help restore the person you love as one who both gives and receives healthy touch.

Feelings

Survivors of child sexual abuse have often gone through life with emotionally numbed feelings as a form of protection against the pain carried within themselves. Since feelings are not selectively numbed—pain, humiliation, anger over the abuse, pleasure, joy—*all* feelings often have become numb. As healing proceeds and feelings begin to come alive again, it is also not all or nothing. The first feelings are often terrible pain and sadness experienced in the remembering stage. If a survivor is able to listen carefully to her inner feelings, she will hear some anger, outrage, and even see some self-respect within that pain. Whatever the first feelings that rise to the surface are, after having been emotionally numb for so long, they are likely to be very intense and often frightening because of their intensity.

> *One woman wished she could just get angry and scream at some form representing her abuser and for months and months she was unable to do so. The next time I saw her and asked how it was going with the anger, she laughed. She reported she had started screaming at a pillow she kept to represent her abuser and felt the anger and the rage flow out. Her laughter, she explained, was that she had done this yelling and screaming for nine straight days. "I wanted anger and I got it and it felt wonderful!"*

As the friend, family member or lover, when the survivor slowly begins to experience her true feelings, offer her lots of reassurances that you are there for her to listen, especially to the feelings most frightening. Understanding the reason behind the feelings the survivor shares with others will help you remain nonjudgmental. This is very important to prevent the survivor from trying to suppress feelings that others do not approve or agree with.

It is very common for survivors to fear their feelings both as a result of the actual abuse experience and also stemming from the healing process itself. After years of emotional numbing, each new feeling may be accompanied with feelings of awe, wonder, fear, even gleeful giggling, as these people truly experience their healing progress. Encourage them to practice experiencing the feelings they are perceiving in the here and now, rather than dissociating when a feeling arises that is frightening. Reassure them that sadness does not necessarily predict the onset of another major depression; anxiety is not necessarily the forerunner to a panic attack. Each are just feelings in the huge spectrum of human feelings that result from reacting to daily life. Help them see that not all feelings are dangerous and need to be suppressed or run away from.

Be supportive as your loved one begins to experience her feelings for the first time and strive to quell her fears through your nonjudgmental support. Plan a way to celebrate each new feeling she experiences to mark her progress. Each new sensation truly experienced is a milestone in her healing journey.

Survivors are frequently convinced that they are loosing their minds as they begin to experience the intensity of some of their feelings. They see their uncontrollable emotions as a sign of helplessness. The perceived helplessness is often believed to be proof of their insanity; that these new feelings have caused them to loose control completely. Help them to see this perceived loss of control is a false perception and that their new feelings are a healthy sign. Emotionally they have begun their own rebirthing. No matter how frightening initially, experiencing their emotions is far better than numbing themselves to their inner-most feelings. Repeatedly reassure survivors that these shows of intense emotions are not a sign of losing control, that they are far from demonstrations of helplessness, and that any problems they are experiencing are only temporary. These feelings are proof that the survivor is truly healing and becoming whole once again.

At first it may be difficult for the survivor to discriminate when the expression of certain feelings is appropriate. She may fly into a rage in the grocery store if there is no whipped cream or she may become very depressed if someone does not like her new haircut. These extreme demonstrations of emotion can be very distressing to the survivor who often thinks she is out of control, one of her deepest fears. She is not loosing control. The situation is just the opposite. The survivor is in the process of learning how and where she chooses to express or control her feelings, much in the way small children do when they discover their own feelings. Her feelings have been repressed and numbed for so long that now she is discovering them for the first time. The emotional reactions stem from the newness of experiencing feelings and, while these reactions do sometimes cause embarrassment, they also provide valuable practice in discriminating when and how to express feelings.

Once the survivor is reassured that these exaggerated displays of emotions will not last forever but exist to help her learn healthy control of her expressions of emotion, she begins to return to a life free of emotional numbness. As adults we often grow impatient, and the survivor does too. Remember that the learning taking place here involves both an adult and small child and, if patience cannot yet be mustered for the adult, concentrate on the child. We often possess far greater patience and understanding for the repetition and practice involved in children's learning. It is in allowing the child to experience all of his/her feelings and to practice expressing them that the child discovers how to appropriately express him/herself—a skill carried forward throughout life. This is the process the survivor was deprived of as a child victim of sexual abuse. Learning to experience and exercise control over her emotions is what the survivor now struggles to achieve.

Anger

Anger is an essential component of the healing process and one that many people, women in particular, may fear. This fear is often based on traditional instruction that says angry women are abnormal or treacherous beings. Still others fear that should their intense anger ever rise to the surface it would be horribly destructive and they would have no control over it. For the survivor, anger is the healthy response to the violation of sexual abuse, and its expression creates a powerful positive energy. The adult survivor needs to learn what anger is and how she can experience and express this human emotion without it getting out of control and harming others or herself.

At the time of the abuse, the child may have been unable to experience her anger or to express it. Anger left unexpressed is like an inner poison; it will fester, grow into rage and be directed indiscriminately. For many survivors, this anger is directed inward—

at the child part of them they have blamed for the abuse and have learned to hate for their vulnerability. Depression and other self-destructive behavior stems from this inwardly directed anger (depression = anger turned inward).

Your loved one needs your help to see that this kind of anger punishes the child within her for having done no wrong. Point out that this anger punishes the child for being vulnerable, injured, unable to protect herself. She punishes herself for merely being what a child naturally is.

Helping the survivor acknowledge that the child victim is not deserving of her anger is the first step. The second step is to make anger safe by demonstrating healthy anger. Express your anger verbally as it naturally arises throughout the healing process: "I feel angry because..." This helps the survivor learn a new model of anger that is not abusive. It also demonstrates that you can have and share your feelings of anger; that you're not going to leave her because you are angry. The expression of anger for the survivor then begins to feel safer. Don't expect miracles. This relearning process by the survivor will require many repetitions. Remember that her trust is badly shaken. Keeping this in mind will stop you from showing anger that can have detrimental effects on the survivor; modeling anger that is unsafe. In unsafe anger the verbalizations change from "I feel anger..." to "You make me angry..." and are often followed by either threats of leaving or actually walking away from the individual. The survivor's fear that anger is not a safe emotion will often be confirmed in this instance.

The third step is to help her direct her anger where it appropriately belongs—squarely at the abuser. To take this step creates positive healing energy. It finally releases the survivor from her belief that she was responsible for what was done to her and places that responsibility rightfully on the abuser.

Redirecting all the pent-up anger toward the abuser does not have to mean a direct confrontation between survivor and abuser. This task is too overwhelming for many survivors at this stage. Also, in many cases the abuser has died and a confrontation would be impossible. You can help your loved one accomplish the freeing up of their misdirected anger in several ways, two are mentioned here.

A punching bag or a pillow. Using a punching bag or a large pillow, urge your loved one to start punching it as if it were the abuser standing in front of her. Encourage her to tell the abuser how angry she feels, what she feels about the abuser, what she'd like to see happen to him, what she'd like to do to him. Help her get started by using your own feelings toward the abuser. "I hate him for what he did to you. He's despicable and not worthy of any sympathy." Urge the survivor on until her anger begins to flow freely. Expect the survivor's intensity level to escalate as she gets fully in touch with her anger. After reaching a peak many survivors experience complete exhaustion giving way to a calm, cleansed feeling.

Writing a letter. The ritual of writing a letter that is never meant to be sent can accomplish the same release of anger. Once completed, the letter can be retained to remind the survivor, should old anger patterns reappear, who was and is responsible for the abuse. As with the punching bag, the intent is the same. Encourage the survivor to write a letter to the abuser stating everything she feels and thinks about the abuser and what was done to her, both as a child and now as an adult. It is the abuser who is responsible, not the victim. Your encouragement helps the survivor tap into the depths of her anger and allows the anger to flow onto the paper. She can use different colored pens to express different emotions and include pictures, no matter how unprofessionally they may appear, to help her express her feelings.

These ideas represent only two possible options for helping survivors redirect their anger. Be creative, use the materials that you have readily available. Breaking balloons works well, breaking old dishes while wearing protective eye wear has helped some, going to a remote location and screaming everything thought and felt about the abuser is another. To be most helpful be an active participant. Be there to support and encourage the survivor to overcome her long-standing resistance to expressing her deepest anger. The power of this release and the positive healing energy that it creates cannot be over stated. At some point in the healing process this poison that is sickening the survivor must be released so the survivor can begin to reevaluate how she thinks and feels about herself, about who she truly is now that she is no longer the victim.

What if the survivor does not feel any anger? As a result of years of repression and emotional numbing, some survivors may say they do not feel any anger. The slightest sense of angry feelings may seem overpowering and threaten their sense of control. Some survivors feel immense fear of loosing control if they get in touch with their anger. In order to maintain the delicate inner balance, anger is often numbed from experience as a method of helping them maintain a sense of control.

The survivor often fears that to feel even a little of her anger would result in a rage that would never cease and her complete destruction would ensue. This is not a sign that anger does not exist but rather an indication that anger is buried deep within and has only started to rise to the surface. If this is the case with your loved one, there are steps you can take to help her get in touch with her anger when she feels ready to proceed in this direction.

The techniques offered here should be undertaken with great caution and not without the assistance of the survivor's therapist. The danger is that you may be unequipped to handle the emotions that may arise and find yourself and the survivor in a crisis situation. If the survivor is requesting your help in breaking through her denial and reaching her underlying anger, request the survivor's permission to speak to her therapist about the best way to help her and to be prepared to handle whatever emotions may arise. Often it is best that anger in denial is dealt with in a therapeutic setting with a trained professional there to challenge and guide the survivor through her anger. If this is the advice you receive from the survivor's therapist, inform your loved one of your concerns and do not engage in the following techniques. Let the therapist do these activities with your loved one.

- Use a magazine article about a small child, preferably one with pictures. After reading the article aloud, ask the survivor to talk about her feelings. Offer encouragement at all signs of anger that appear as she talks.
- Help the survivor make a list of all of the ways that the abuse has affected her life, both as a child and now as an adult. Then have her read the list aloud two or three times. Ask her to talk about how it feels to read this list. What items begin to stand out and sound angry. Encourage her to say more about these items.

- Using the abuser's name and beginning each statement with "I feel angry . . . " ask the survivor to talk about this person. Prompt her along with phrases like "How much anger do you feel?" and "Why do you feel so angry?" Using this technique allows the survivor to get at the root of her anger because when she says, "I feel angry that he hurt me," and you prompt, "How did he hurt you?" The anger resulting from the abuse begins to manifest itself more freely.
- Shop garage sales for inexpensive breakable dishes. Then ask the survivor to visualize the abuser against a fence or garage wall and begin throwing the dishes at the image saying whatever comes to mind. A word of caution: Make sure that you and the survivor are wearing protective eye wear to avoid injury.

The objective in doing any of these exercises is to help the survivor get in touch with and begin to express all of the angry feelings about the abuse and the abuser. This expression of anger is effectively redirected away from being self-anger, a toxin destroying her from within, to anger that is appropriately placed on the one responsible for the pain. It frees her from anger's grip to heal her wounds. Verbalizing this anger, like breaking the silence of the abuse, is another major step in the healing process. Your complete acceptance of the survivor and her anger is critical. You should prepare yourself to hear the depths of her anger so you do not appear shocked by it and frighten the survivor into repressing her anger again. Seeing your acceptance enables the survivor to begin to accept the rightful anger she holds within and to direct it toward the abuser without feelings of guilt.

Your loved one, like many survivors, may be reluctant to try any of these anger exercises because she fears getting angry or loosing control, fears being embarrassed or rejected. If she was from a dysfunctional family where she witnessed anger that was violent, destructive or out of control, she may have come to believe anger is always this way. In addition, many survivors have spent their entire lives trying to maintain control over themselves and their enviornmnet as a result of the abuse and may fear that to get angry is to loose this precious control. These are very real fears and are not to be treated lightly. Reassure the survivor that anger can be channeled in ways that are healthy and constructive and that it can work as positive energy to help heal the pain. If control is the issue, offer reassurance that you are not afraid she will loose control, that you will be right there with her and that you'll help her express her anger.

One woman with no history of violence in her family was immobilized at the thought of truly experiencing the anger she knew was being held hostage within her. "When I think of him (her father), I begin to feel all of this anger that quickly turns into a blinding rage and my mind fills with images of beating in his face with a baseball bat."

This woman feared that releasing her anger would actually lead her to such violent behavior, a very unlikely possibility. Without the actual release of her anger, the images within her mind became more violent as the poison within her built and she, in turn, became more frightened to release the anger at all.

Another fear is that the anger will be misdirected towards someone close to the survivor because she views her anger as a force that will get out of control and be indiscriminate in its target.

Again you can provide support and encouragement in this situation. With no history of violence, it is very rare for a survivor to act out her anger in violent ways toward her abuser or the others in her immediate proximity. Remind the survivor that the fear she is experiencing is the result of never having had the opportunity to experience or express her outrage as a child being abused. Her years of repressing the anger provided no opportunity to practice and learn that anger can be experienced and expressed without fear and directed, with control, to meet her needs. We seldom consciously think of anger as a skill that requires practice, but that is what it is. This practice is exactly what a two- or three-year-old child is doing when testing parental limits in a healthy family. It is through this practice that the child learns to express anger appropriately. The child sexual abuse survivor was denied the opportunity to practice expressing anger. She may need many reassurances now that she deserves the opportunity to begin practicing experiencing and expressing her anger now.

Without practicing and eventually releasing all of this stored up anger, the survivor will remain stuck in this most unpleasant place and never achieve the joys that resolution holds out to her. Anger either acts like a dam, holding back the dirty, stale flood waters that stifle the river of life, or anger acts like a lock and dam system opening the gates enough to allow the stale water to flow out and mix with the new to form the river of a life moving towards its fulfillment. The task may not be an easy one, but if you support the survivor in her anger, help her find ways to release some of it and applaud her bravery, you both will be able to see the steps she is taking toward healing. You and the survivor will find great joy in the new life that emerges when feelings are free to be experienced and expressed.

Grief and mourning

> *"I don't think it's possible to die from crying, but after two weeks of seemingly endless tears, I was sure it was indeed possible. I wasn't even able to explain to anyone the reasons for all my tears; they just kept coming."*

The endless tears were so overwhelming that this woman's exact grief got lost in a sea of losses she experienced that were all surfacing and being mourned simultaneously.

The survivor of child sexual abuse has many losses to mourn: the loss of innocence, of a childhood, of the ability to trust, of having a secure sense of self, of the ability to experience the fullness of their feelings, their sexuality. This list is not nearly complete but serves to illustrate the overwhelming losses incurred as a result of child sexual abuse—losses from childhood well into adulthood. It provides a clear understanding of the depth and intensity of the tears shed by the survivor when remembering and realizing the cost she has paid for events that were perpetrated against her as a child.

Grief that is not shared acts much like anger not expressed; it becomes an inner poison affecting a person's ability to experience joy or pleasure in life. For the child victim, grieving the traumatic experience was often not possible and, as a result, all those feelings of loss were numbed—but they were not eliminated. The deep feelings of loss still exist within the adult survivor. The poison needs to be purged by sharing and expressing the grief, by mourning the losses which began in childhood and have continued into the present.

Helping the survivor through this stage can be especially difficult. To truly release these feelings, the survivor must travel back to that traumatic time, reliving some of the experiences of the abuse. Enduring the emotional pain permits the transformation of grief into a positive healing experience as the losses are named, shared and reduced to being a small part of the survivor's life rather than an all-consuming theme.

To help your loved one mourn her losses requires little of you in the way of direct action, but it requires much of your capability to withstand seeing, hearing and feeling another's deepest pain. Your role is to listen supportively, to honor and respect both the individual and her shared feelings, and to validate all losses as real and worthy of being mourned. Your openness to this process will help the survivor begin the grieving process. Your continued support and empathy will act as encouragement to proceed despite the pain that is involved in doing so.

Grieving, like remembering, cannot be contained within the constraints of time. It does not start on a given date and end at the appropriately appointed time. Grieving requires time and space. The survivor cannot assign a time during which she will grieve or set aside a day to remember the childhood trauma and grieve for it. An adult survivor may grieve very intensely for a week and then go for a month without further mourning and then begin again. As a person committed to helping a survivor, you need to respect the time that grieving requires. To urge your loved one to speed up the process, to get on with it, to get it over with, is futile and only serves to invalidate her feelings. Knowing this, you may need to remind your loved one that she is on a journey that has no shortcuts and cannot be rushed. Remind her that an afternoon spent in tears grieving her losses is not sufficient to mourn all of the losses that have been accrued over a lifetime. Remind the survivor that she deserves the gift of time, space and support to grieve her very real losses and that you are there to insure that these gifts are not taken away.

Sometimes a survivor may have difficulty connecting the impact of the child sexual abuse with losses extending beyond childhood, losses which also need to be grieved. As someone who knows the survivor, you may be able to help her make all of these connections possible. This may include missing out on school dances and dating due to fear and shame, an inability to form close lasting interpersonal relationships, the loss of a grandfather for their own children. The list could be endless. The point is to make every effort to help the survivor uncover all of this hidden grief at a pace she determines.

Depression may ebb and flow as the survivor goes in and out of different periods of mourning. The grieving process involves a natural period of sadness often accompanied by a low energy level, social withdrawal and a lessened concern with outside activities. Encourage the survivor to accept some depression, acknowledging it as the normal and temporary process of grieving, and arrange for her to have as much companionship as possible during and immediately following a period of depression.

Anxiety

Anxiety is commonly experienced by survivors of child sexual abuse. The roots of this anxiety are in the fear experienced at the actual time of the abuse and the fear that continues to grow until the abuse issued are resolved. The survivor may experience occasional anxious feelings or may be in a constant state of anxiety including severe panic attacks. Panic attacks include excessive perspiration, sensations of difficulty in breathing, rapid heartbeat, feelings of dizziness and a sense of impending doom. The state of anxiety may be related to a specific fear or, over time, it may have developed into a generalized state of anxiety in which the survivor remains hypersensitive and feels anxious most of the time, regardless of the situation. Common anxieties and fears reported by survivors include fear of

- Being in crowded places.
- Entering stores, standing in line.
- Traveling, accidents, getting lost.
- Collapsing, fainting, getting sick, becoming paralyzed and unable to escape the situation.
- Going "crazy," harming someone else.

Survivors may feel very confused over their anxiety. They may ask themselves or others "What is going on? Why am I feeling this way?" With the confusion caused by this type of anxiety, survivors may not be able to identify the source of stress at the time it occurs.

This inability to determine the "cause" of the anxiety frequently creates a viscous cycle of escalating fear. Unable to identify the cause, survivors may suddenly depart from a social situation and rush home. In the following weeks they may remain isolated as shey become increasingly afraid of leaving home for fear of experiencing another anxiety attack in public.

To overcome feelings of anxiety, it is necessary for the survivor to begin to identify the sources causing the stress. Unresolved issues surrounding sexual abuse are often uncovered in the therapy process. The survivor may have an unconscious fear of being assaulted while in public. She may feel everyone around her knows or will find out about her abuse. Whatever the source, once identified the survivor may need your help and support to face the situations which produce these states of anxiety.

You can help the survivor by reminding her that her fears are a natural response to a situation she finds stressful, that it is not an indication that there is something wrong with her. When the fear can be identified as having its roots in abuse issues, remind the survivor that she is safe now; she is no longer a small child unable to protect herself from the world around her. Since fear often results in the survivor's preparation to flee the situation in an escalation of anxiety, encourage the survivor to *float*, not to fight her feeling of fear. Remind her that these feelings will pass if no resistance is mounted.

Encourage the survivor to verbalize her worst fears surrounding the anxiety producing situation. For example, if the survivor becomes afraid of passing out in a store, ask her, "What is the worst thing that could happen if this actually occured?" Frequently the survivor will state how embarrassed she would feel, that "everyone" would know her secret, that she will get lost and be unable to find her way out of the situation, or that these terrible feelings will never leave her. Help the survivor assess her thought processes and evaluate their appropriateness. A common reaction to anxiety is for the survivor to catastrophize: to imagine the very worst that could happen if her anxiety manifested itself. These catastrophic consequences are rarely realized. Once the survivor can be assisted to understand this she can respond to anxiety and fear with the internal advise of, "So what—do it anyway. It will pass."

This does not suggest that the survivor ignore her fears and anxiety but rather that she develop skills for assessing the real from the imagined. For instance, if the survivor is in a situation where she feels she is being followed and is in potential danger, it is important that she has the skills to distinguish between this real, appropriate fear and her other destructive anxiety.

Issues of control in the adult survivor

As a small child being sexually abused, the survivor lost all control over her life. It was the abuser who decided how and when her small body was to be used to meet his/her needs. The child lost control of all choices, rights and arguments on her own behalf and through the survival mechanisms of denial, dissociation and emotional numbing, she instilled strict control over her physical and emotional reactions to manage her inner pain. It should not come as a surprise that many adult survivors present strong control issues which may affect everyone around them. These issues can be very difficult to tolerate and will tax your limits at times. Remembering the tragic loss of control sustained as a child will help you to understand and assist the adult survivor who has a strong need for control as she continues her recovery.

Physical control

Many adult survivors felt completely unable to predict or control the events in their lives during the period of the abuse. One response to these feelings was to continue to live as though they remained helpless against the abuse, and this response was then generalized across others areas of their lives. This helplessness is noted by a general passivity that survivors just aren't strong enough and the belief that they are victims by their very nature. Helpless survivors are likely to attribute any misfortune to internal causes: "I should have known better." They also tend to generalize their situation: "Someone is always out to abuse me wherever I go." This sense of helplessness is very dangerous because it leaves the survivor open to continuously feeling revictimized. As adults, survivors are continuing to act as children who have not learn how to say no nor how to protect themselves. What they know is how to be controlled, victimized, abused and they feel helpless to change this.

As friends, family members or lovers you can help your loved one work to overcome this helplessness in several ways. One way is to challenge the helpless explanations whenever you hear them. Counter her "I should have's" when she speaks of the abuse with statements that directly place all of the blame for the abuse on the abuser and completely away from her. For example, if the survivor states, "I should have come right home from school. If I would have, this wouldn't have happened." Counter her statement with something like, "Being late from school does not give anyone the right to abuse you. You didn't do anything wrong." Remind her to consider what realistic expectations of a child are. Use a small child of your own or one the survivor knows to help her think about this concretely.

> Sarah was deeply involved in trying to help her friend Karen to heal the wounds of her child sexual abuse. Karen began to speak more and more of what she should have done on her own behalf when the abuse began at age nine.
>
> One day, while the two of them watched Sarah's eight-year-old daughter in the pool, Sarah challenged Karen to really look at her, to look at her small size, her fragile muscles, her trusting attitude. After a brief time, Sarah asked Karen what she thought this eight-year-old young girl could realistically do if Sarah's husband decided to enter her room at night and sexually abuse her. Karen broke down and sobbed. She realized how helpless this small child would be in that situation. She became aware that there wasn't anything she could do against such a large adult, just like there wasn't anything Karen "should" have been able to do against her own abuser.

Such a revelation is not always this easy to obtain but if you are persistent and gentle in your challenges of the survivor's explanations, you can assist her to break free of her helpless feelings.

You can also gently confront the survivor's generalized belief that she simply is not strong enough and was essentially born to be a victim with concrete examples to the contrary. Remind her of specific instances, both in the past and now, where the survivor has clearly acted as a strong individual. Believing in her helplessness, the survivor may passively argue with you presenting "Yes, but . . . " arguments to substantiate her view of herself as a victim because even though terribly painful, it is frightening to change this view. Be persistent. Don't give up your gentle challenges.

Emotional control

When the fear and pain of the sexual abuse became too devastating to experience directly, victims frequently exerted extreme control over their emotions and continue to do so into adulthood. They may lie to themselves and others about their feelings or deny them altogether. They are harshly judgmental about themselves, take themselves and life very seriously, and are unable to have fun or find joy in anything. Frequently survivors will overreact in any situations they perceive as being out of their control.

These self-controlling patterns are a response to the abusive situation when the survivor experienced a loss of all control herself. The survivor often believes her protective mechanism will prevent a loss of control from ever occurring again. Try and accept your loved one's need for this control and express your understanding of the connection between this current behavior and the abuse. This can encourage the survivor to try new, less self-controlling behaviors because you have created a safe place for her to take risks without fearing judgment or rejection. This is not the time to confront or challenge the survivor on any issues. Doing so may be very threatening to the survivor who fears losing control, and your confrontation or challenge may be perceived as another form of abuse which may strengthen the victim role.

For many survivors it is very difficult to become less rigid, more tolerant of change, and less judgmental of themselves and others. It is frightening to abandon the belief that remaining in emotional control of themselves will keep them safe from further abuse. Helping your loved one to make minor changes and to admit small errors without becoming very angry at herself can help her begin to break her pattern of emotional control. Reinforce each small change she is able to accomplish. Commend her on her new level of self-acceptance and tolerance, and acknowledge how difficult a task she has undertaken and how well she is progressing toward mastery of that task.

Manipulating behaviors

Some survivors turn to manipulating others around them in order to gain a sense of control. These patterns interfere with the healing process by decreasing social interaction and increasing the survivor's isolation. In addition, attempting to control others requires the expenditure of a great deal of energy trying to determine what their reactions will be. This energy is then depleted from that which is available for healing tasks.

For friends, family members and lovers it is important to recognize these manipulative patterns as a misdirected attempt at protection rather than as malicious acts against you. This recognition will help you react in a context of acceptance and understanding rather than with anger and a judgmental attitude. While your acceptance and understanding is very important, you do not have to feel abused yourself while the survivor works on relearning these patterns in therapy.

One woman I interviewed reported feeling terribly abused by the friend she was trying to help. Whenever the woman offered verbal reinforcement of the survivor's attempts to heal, the survivor would retort, "You're just like my father (the abuser), telling me how sweet and good I am all the time."

Needless to say, this woman was devastated by these remarks. In addition to hurting her friend deeply, this survivor's manipulative behavior was effective in protecting her from recognizing or discussing the positive healing steps she had taken. Be honest but supportive about your reaction to this kind of manipulative behavior.

These are not contradictory terms; be honest about your feelings and supportive of the survivor. As an example, you may say, "I feel deeply hurt when you compare me to your father who abused you as a child, but I support your letting me know that you're feeling threatened right now." You can be both supportive and understanding without sacrificing yourself and your feelings for the healing of another. To deny your own feelings in a manipulative situation and to think the survivor is too fragile to hear your truthful communication harms both of you. If you deny your own feelings, you will begin to build a surplus of resentment that will render you unable to assist the survivor in the healing process. To consider the survivor too fragile for truthful communications relegates her back to the role of victim, a role she is struggling to leave behind. Neither denying your feelings or protecting the survivor from them has a place in the healing process.

Manipulative patterns can present you with a difficult challenge. Try and remember the three points covered in the section on "Taking care of yourself."
- Set your limits.
- Communicate them to the survivor.
- Advise the survivor when you are getting close to reaching your limits.

Making changes

The concept of survivors having to make life changes may puzzle some since throughout this book it has been emphasized that the victims/survivors didn't do anything wrong; that they are not to blame for the abuse, and this is true. What they did do unconsciously for their survival however, was to develop inappropriate behaviors and attitudes linked to the abuse experience, behaviors that have become so natural that changing them requires substantial effort and support.

As the survivor begins to make changes, there may repercussions from those around her. It is not uncommon or unhealthy if you find yourself feeling a little threatened as the survivor starts to make changes. Even if the changes are for the better for the survivor and for your relationship with her, it is part of human nature to prefer the familiar over the new and unknown. Remember that the survivor shares your fears, and together you can work on changes that will result in a healthier life for both of you. To do this, address your fears and then get them out in the open for honest discussion.

An example that may serve as clarification here is that both you and your loved one may share a fear about what change will mean to your feelings. The survivor's fears may center around how she will handle all of her true feelings since she is familiar only with numbed feelings designed as a wall of protection. You may fear her change to real feelings will result in the lessening of feelings that the survivor has held for you. Both are unnecessary fears that can hamper the commitment to change. If the survivor changes to a life of experiencing and expressing real feelings, far less energy will be spent erecting and maintaining her wall of protection and more energy can be directed toward experiencing all the joyous feelings of life. For the friend, family member or lover, the survivor has had strong feelings for you in an emotionally numbed state; after positive change, the reality and strength of those feelings will tend to increase as her feelings become truly real. Change may be scary but it need not stop either of you from working together to achieve it.

Change is difficult. Old behavioral patterns are very strong and they fight back when threatened. It is very common that a pattern of behavior will resist change the strongest just when it is about to give way. A survivor struggling to change her binge eating patterns may be doing very well and suddenly have an entire day of bingeing. The old pattern is fighting for its survival. The survivor needs your encouragement at these times to keep working to change an old pattern that doesn't want to give up. The survivor may feel depressed that all of her efforts will never pay off. Remind her how well she has been doing and that one slip cannot erase all of her hard work and progress. Let her know you're with her and that you support all of her efforts.

The one change survivors may find most frightening and you may find yourself most threatened by is their learning to set boundaries; to put themselves first; to say no. The child victim was never given the opportunity to say no and therefore never learned how to set appropriate boundaries for herself that serve and protect her. Survivors need to learn to say no and to practice saying no, beginning with small and insignificant things. You can allow, encourage and respect the survivor's efforts to become more assertive.

Boundaries are those invisible lines we draw around ourselves that delineate where "I stop and you begin." They may be widely drawn or held very close to our physiology and neither is more correct. In addition we all hold several boundaries all at once. We allow some people to get close to us while others are held at bay. What is important about our boundaries is that they are determined by each of us and they serve as a form of protection and a warning system. If someone begins to infringe upon our boundaries—let's assume they start telling us what to do or think—our projection of who we are is threatened and a warning is sounded that says, "No, that's not what I want to do nor is that what I want to think."

Our boundaries protect the integrity of who we are. For child sexual abuse survivors, boundaries can be easily penetrated by others because their sense of self and their self-esteem is so low. What others think, do and say is perceived as more important and better than what the survivor thinks. These permeable boundaries allow everything in because there is no sense of self and, therefore, no warning system to advise the survivor of trespassers so that she may elicit a negative response. To feel good about one's self, a person must have the capacity to set limits. The greatest incentive to struggle through this challenge is in knowing that, as survivors set protective limits, they also give themselves more freedom to be who they truly are, rather than who someone else thinks or says they should be.

One of the best tools to assist the survivor with this difficult challenge is role-playing. Begin with the least threatening person or situation in the survivor's life and slowly move up the those more personal and frightening.

For example,
- You play a casual friend who is telling the survivor that she is putting her tomato plants in all wrong. Tell the survivor that you'll be over to show her how to do it "right."
- It is early in the morning and the grocery store has just opened. You play a female store customer who crowds in front of the survivor in the checkout line with the argument that, because of her full basket, she obviously got to the store just when it opened and deserves to go first.
- You play the survivor's employer who tells her to stay late because he's not quite ready with the material for tomorrow's meeting.
- You play the survivor's spouse who feels sexual tonight, but the survivor does not.

In each example the survivor should focus on
- What feelings arise
- How difficult it is to say no.

Discuss each one, or reverse roles so the survivor can observe you model the same situations.

New patterns of saying no will not be met with applause by those who prefer the "old" victim, but many others will applaud as a survivor begins to take better care of herself at last. Remind your loved one that all change is met with both approval and disapproval, but the ultimate approval belongs within herself. When she can say no she won't find herself in unwanted relationships, she will no longer feel like a victim, and she will experience far more self-esteem, confidence and power than she ever thought possible. These are the gains that make the difficult task of change worth all of the work and more.

Recovery: slips and slides

As I have said over and over, healing the wounds from child sexual abuse is an on-going process, one that continues for life. This is not to convey a message of hopelessness that all of the steps of remembering, anger, crisis, depression and disassociation continue at the same intensity and frequency throughout the healing process. The intent is to alert you to the reality that slips and slides backward do occur in the healing process. As the friend, family member or lover you can help the survivor by being aware of this potential and understanding that it is perfectly normal and temporary. After all, even those of us who were not abused know the feeling that comes over us when we suddenly remember an unpleasant event from our past. If the unpleasant memory arises and the entire day is disrupted, the memory is to blame. This is the same phenomenon for the survivor.

Slips and slides may be short or long, and the survivor may return to one of the earlier stages of healing. Events, situations, certain people, a newspaper article on child abuse, hearing that someone the survivor knows has just begun his/her own process of remembering—these are all items which can trigger a slip. In a flash the survivor begins to reexperience her own abuse; this time after having gone through one or several of the painful processes of healing. She not only feels the fear experienced as a child victim but now a new fear enters: This short relapse may signal that she must begin the recovery process all over again. Reassure the survivor that this is not true. Remind her that slips are only small steps backwards in the healing process in which she has already taken many more steps forward. Slips and slides back in the healing process will not last forever; they will pass. Remind the survivor how she has survived other difficult times and reassure her that this difficult time will also pass.

It is important to know that a relapse does not take the survivor back to the beginning of the healing process. Quite the contrary, it is more like people tripping when they walk down the sidewalk. They may sway back and forth and try to regain their balance and generally, most do—with only a few actually falling. If you can keep this in mind and remind the survivor of it during a slip, you will be of tremendous help in reassuring and helping her to calm her fears.

Having gone through the long and very painful healing process, it is not surprising that a relapse could strike terror in the heart of the survivor. She has cried, struggled, screamed, felt unbearable pain and, just as she is beginning to feel better, along comes a slide. Her terror may begin to manifest itself as panic with symptoms very much the same as those experienced in the earlier stages: anxiety, fear, lack of concentration. In addition she may have feelings of sadness, anger and powerlessness accompanying the memory or situation that has touched the old wounds. With all of this emotional information flooding in, the survivor quite naturally may believe that the process is starting all over again, that she can't regain her balance, that she will indeed fall.

Reassure her, repeatedly if necessary, that this is not the case. Encourage the survivor to view this as a temporary slip that can be looked at and discussed to uncover the connection between what she remembered or experienced now that reminded her of the abuse of the past. The capacity to make these connections between now and then is significant because, once made, the past and present are no longer fused together as one, as they were in earlier stages. The survivor can see the present as separate from the memory of the past and know that she now has the power to maintain that separation. The past need never totally envelop her again.

Anniversary dates are especially difficult for many survivors and may trigger a slip backward: dates, such as when the survivors first began to remember, when they entered therapy, when they first revealed their secret to someone. The sensitivity to these dates stems from two different points. One, they serve as reminders of a very painful time, a time not yet that far removed from where the survivor currently is and they can elicit the fear that the survivor will return to that painful point in her healing process. The second stems from being reminded how long the healing process is taking and may prompt negative thinking such as "I should be better by now." If you are able, help the survivor plan ahead for these dates. Make anniversaries special days with the survivor where you celebrate her on-going recovery, recognizing all of the progress she has made. Reassure her that feeling depressed on these anniversary dates does not signal a return to the very early painful days but is a natural response to the losses she has experienced, including the time it is now taking to heal.

One woman shared the idea of making up a calendar marking all the days that were potential triggers for her. Once the calendar had been assembled, the survivor had a visual reminder that some rough days lay ahead and that preparation was in order. Survivors may choose to spend time with a close and trusted friend that day or plan an activity that will overshadow the reminder that day holds for them. Knowing an emotionally loaded day is coming and making plans for it helps reduce or minimize a potential slip. These methods are not foolproof nor do they offer protection from very powerful emotional days, but they are effective in many instances and can reserve the survivor's energy resources for the most difficult times.

Holidays and other special occasions can all be especially vulnerable times for the survivor with strained or severed family ties. From birth we are taught that these are times when families come together to celebrate or to mourn. This may be the first time that the survivor has insisted on what she needs by refusing to attend a family function and, in turn, she may experience feelings of guilt. It can be a time of profound loneliness, sadness or even suicidal thoughts because refusal to attend a gathering is a reminder of the loss of an ideal she held dear for a lifetime—that her family was wonderful. In the midst of this distress, the survivor may be tempted to let her guidelines for taking care of her own needs slide and participate in the holiday in the "old familiar" way. Unless enough time has passed and she is truly ready to revise her guidelines, spend time talking to the survivor about her intentions and what purpose she sees in carrying them out.

To ease the pain when the survivor is going to be alone on special occasions, brainstorm with the survivor for alternative activities for the day of the family get-together.

- If the survivor is a friend, not a lover or spouse, can the survivor spend the holiday with you and your family?

- If you're both unattached, plan a dinner out followed by an activity associated with the occasion you're celebrating: i.e. ice skating, sledding, skiing or caroling for Christmas, attending the temple for Hanukkah or church for Easter, or going to a parade or band concert on the Fourth of July.
- Encourage the survivor to volunteer helping others celebrate the holiday: i.e. helping to cook a feast, collecting money or food for the needy, decorating a space.
- If the survivor is your lover or spouse, begin a new tradition that strives to meet the survivor's desire to mark the occasion and try to make it a yearly tradition. Celebrate with your own children, if you have them, and friends in your immediate circle.

Forgive and forget

Untold numbers of survivors have suffered additional and unnecessary pain and distress by having a friend, family member, or lover advise them to "forgive and forget, after all, the abuse occurred a long time ago." Whether the abuse occurred a long time ago or yesterday, this advice minimizes what did occur and its lasting impact upon the life of the survivor. "Forgive and forget" denies the validity of the feelings the survivor is experiencing because they could not be expressed at the time of the abuse.

Some in the Judeo-Christian tradition refer to scriptures that speak of one's sacred duty to forgive. A very common mistake in cases where the abuser was a member of the clergy is to ask the victim to forgive the perpetrator. The Rev. Marie Fortune, in an analysis of Christian forgiving, points out that the divine power of God may forgive the abuser, not the victim's forgiveness.[1] The victim in all cases is due an apology—not religious pressure to forgive the perpetrator. If in healing, the victim finds forgiveness, that is fine, but attempting to pressure him/her to forgive the abuser often leads to increased feelings that he/she is truly "bad" because no forgiveness can be found.

The only forgiveness that counts in the healing process is that which the survivor finds for him/herself. When a child is sexually abused, that experience and the small abused child become frozen in time due to the overwhelming impact the abuse has on that young life.

As the child grows into adolescence and adulthood, he/she continues to carry this young child within. For many survivors it has been this young inner child who has been the target of their self-hate and anger. It was this child who caused the abuse, who was vulnerable, who trusted when he/she shouldn't have. As an adult survivor, it has been this child that all self-destructive behavior has been intended to destroy, all without conscious awareness due to the powers of repression.

This inner child is more than a theoretical concept. Many survivors speak clearly of the split they feel between the adult they are on the outside and the scared little child they are inside. This split keeps the child alienated from the rest of the survivor. It is akin to having a mystery novel without the chapter containing the crime; a story incapable of being understood. One survivor described her split as, "Inside I just felt real small and the thing I wanted most of all was for someone to just pick me up and hold me, to comfort me, and just love me. Outside I'm the strong one who can handle anything and doesn't need anyone for anything. I don't want anyone to even try and touch me. I hate weak little things."

The forgiveness that matters is for the survivor to learn to forgive that small, vulnerable child within who could not protect him/herself for the self-destructive behaviors developed to destroy this child, for the failed relationships as an adult, for needing the time to heal this child now. This constitutes what the survivor must learn to forgive in order to fully heal.

Helping the survivor develop self-forgiveness begins when you discard any notion that he/she should "forgive and forget" and when you share that resolution with the survivor. Sharing this decision will remove any perceptions and pressures that *you believe and expect* the victim to forgive the abuser.

Learning to forgive oneself takes time and practice. If the survivor is engaged in negative self-talk: "You're so stupid. I hate you," help her become more aware of it and learn to substitute self-forgiving talk in its place: "Well, you made a mistake, everyone does." Negative self-talk becomes automatic and is often outside of the awareness of the survivor, even though she may say it aloud so you actually hear it. If you should hear the survivor verbalize negative self-talk, it may provide a unique opportunity to help her become more aware of how she talks to herself. Encourage her to figure out alternatives to say to herself in that situation.

One woman who lived alone said she used lots of Post-it-Notes. She wrote affirmations for herself and her inner-child and stuck the notes up throughout the house. "Everywhere I turned there was a note saying, I am loveable, I didn't do anything wrong, I am a good person."

Remind the survivor often how far she has come, that she truly is making progress, that she is healing herself. This reinforces the positive statements she can make to herself and also speaks to her as a survivor rather than a victim. As the occasions of forgiving talk begin to outnumber the occasions of negative self-talk, plan a special celebration to honor the survivor and her progress toward healing—her forgiveness of herself.

Special topics

An Interesting Gentleman
I met him today . . .
    An interesting gentlemen of great stature
With a glowing face
And the beard of my childhood Santa Claus.

He spoke of a will,
A strong desire to live with quality and meaning.

I was captivated by this Santa.
I was horrified by this Santa.
His warmth told me he spoke the truth,
A truth I longed to embrace.

This kind, soft-spoken man
Kindled in me a particle of hope . . .
A small flicker to be developed . . .
Expanded on, somehow.

Each relationship is a blessing to be cherished.
A wonderful gift to receive.
Today I took a baby step to continue with my life,
When I met an interesting gentleman
Who listened and believed.

I strive now not to lose sight
Of this great wonderful gift.

Confrontation

Some survivors, after listening to others who have confronted their abuser, believe that confrontation is something all survivors must do in order to heal themselves. This is not true. Confrontation of the abuser is not necessarily a component in the healing process.

But, if the survivor is considering confrontation, personal reasons for either choosing to confront or not are most important. If the survivor expects validation of the abuse that took place and a demonstration of remorse by the abuser, confrontation is not being done for healthy reasons. Feeling this need for validation denies what the survivor knows to be true, and it undermines the sense of self-trust being developed. Although in some cases the perpetrator may take responsibility for the crime and show remorse and compassion toward the survivor, there is a high likelihood that he will defend himself with denial and anger and blame the survivor. The survivor must be carefully prepared for the worst. Talk to your loved one about the motives for wanting a confrontation and point out any that are not good, healthy reasons for her. And also point out that she may experience the pain of the backlash when her expectations are not met.

One reason some survivors decide to confront their abuser is a type of magical thinking—hoping that when the abuser realizes the pain he has caused the survivor, he will admit his guilt, break down with copious apology, and finally love her. Highly unlikely. If the abuser was disrespectful, unloving, angry and blaming in the past, it is unlikely that his reaction will be different in the present. The survivor will be damaged by a confrontation done for this reason.

The important fact about any confrontation is that it be undertaken realistically; with the mechanics of the confrontation focused entirely on the survivor, not the abuser; and without expectation of a response from the abuser based on what the survivor would *ideally* like to receive. The survivor is capable of controlling only her own responses, not those of anyone else. Assist the survivor by asking her to imagine the worst that could happen as a result of confronting the perpetrator. Generally, survivors will mention denial, anger and blame, but sometimes they fear physical or sexual violence. In such cases, the potential for violence should be taken seriously, and the survivor needs to be sure that the setting for the confrontation is physically safe for her. Help the survivor by asking what she would need to protect herself from the possibility of these "worst fears," both physically and psychologically.

Remember that some survivors have highly developed dissociative abilities as a result of the original abuse. Because of these abilities, the survivor is at maximum risk for dissociation while under the stress of confronting the abuser. It is important that the survivor be given the opportunity to rehearse the confrontation and be encouraged to identify what she needs to protect herself while in the situation.

A reminder of reality is also helpful for many survivors. These reminders may take the form of a message carried in her pocket or an object that reminds her of comfort and security. These reminders can help significantly to ensure that the survivor maintains a reliable connection to herself during the confrontation and should be utilized during rehearsals.

Also you might ask, "What do you need to remember to tell yourself in order to feel okay?" Below are questions assembled by Ellen Bass and Laura Davis in their book, *The Courage To Heal,* to help a survivor make up her mind whether or not to confront the abuser.

1. Whom exactly do I want to talk to? Why?
2. What do I hope to gain from this confrontation? Are my expectations realistic?
3. What are my motives for confronting?
4. Is there anyone who can give me the information I need?
5. What do I stand to gain? To lose?
6. Am I stable and centered enough to risk being called crazy?
7. Could I maintain my own reality in the face of total denial?
8. Can I withstand the anger I am likely to face?
9. Could I handle no reaction at all?
10. Do I have a solid enough support system to back me up before, during and after the confrontation?
11. Have I prepared for the confrontation?

Your loved one trusts you. Suggest that the two of you sit down and go through this list, taking each question very seriously and arrive at an answer uniquely suited for her. If at the end, the survivor has decided against confrontation, remind her that there is no shame in her decision. To confront or not to confront is up to each individual; it is not a requirement of healing. The decision of the survivor, whatever it is, should be respected. The only requirement is that the decision be made carefully and carried out in the best way to allow the survivor to assert her own rights as a person very capable of making this decision.

If after answering the above questions and deciding that a confrontation is what the survivor wants to pursue, it is time to prepare for the meeting. Preparation includes insuring that the survivor is stable and centered, has considered all the possible outcomes and how each of them may impact her life.

As a child victim, the survivor was not met with sympathy or remorse, and to expect such responses now often proves unrealistic. The goal needs to be one where the survivor has the opportunity to say what she needs to say to the abuser about what was done to her and how she feels about it and the abuser, and a direct transfer of responsibility of blame to the abuser. If that is the goal and the survivor keeps to her plan, regardless of the angry defensive response she may receive from the abuser, the survivor has achieved her objective and has taken a giant step in proving to herself and the abuser that she is no longer that vulnerable little child that has so long ruled her life.

All confrontations should be well planned, keeping the needs of the survivor as the primary focus. If an incestuous father agrees to meet but wants to meet in the home of the survivor's childhood, this is not a safe place. The survivor should decline and insist on a meeting place that is either neutral or biased toward the survivor. The survivor should set the time and the limits for the meeting. Meeting with an abusing uncle and his new wife would not be acceptable, and the survivor has the right to ask that only the uncle be present. The terms of the confrontation are in the hands of the survivor.

You can further assist her to be as prepared as possible by helping her in assessing her own level of strength before scheduling the meeting. Full preparation is the best practice for the survivor's emotional well-being before, during and after the confrontation.

Here are some suggestions to help your loved one be prepared.

- Discuss in concrete terms what the objectives are for the meeting and weed out any that do not directly serve the healthy needs of the survivor.
- Discuss the timing, boundaries and location for the meeting. How can these be best insured during the actual meeting?
- Brainstorm all the possible responses you both think may come from the abuser. When you have done this, role play each one, practice what the survivor will say in response to the abuser. Practice until the survivor feels comfortable and confident to withstand whatever the abuser may throw her way.
- Discuss and reaffirm that a confrontation is not a necessary component for recovery. If the survivor begins to have second thoughts, she can put off the confrontation or cancel it altogether without feelings of shame.
- Discuss whether or not the survivor would like you to accompany her to the confrontation as moral support. Confronting the abuser is a very difficult task. Often having someone there who is trusted and knows all the pain, work and effort that has gone into reaching this point can be a tremendous source of strength.

The actual confrontation

The survivor cannot feel psychologically or physically safe if she lacks protection and support. Any child sexual abuser confrontation, especially those involving family members, has the potential of pulling the survivor back into the child role where she began to doubt her reality. As a friend, family or lover you can play an instrumental role by providing support as well as accompanying her to the confrontation. Your presence can be a visual reality she can check to maintain connection with the present and her inner resources. Under no circumstances should the survivor put herself at risk by making the confrontation alone in a place where the perpetrator could abuse her again.

The confrontation is for the survivor. If she has requests from the abuser, this is the time to state them directly even if there are no guarantees that the abuser will comply. The survivor may want an concrete responses such as reimbursement for therapy costs incurred because of the abuse. It is the survivor's time, not the abuser's. The survivor needn't feel obligated to become engaged in a discussion with the abuser. There will always be time for additional dialogue if it is desired by the survivor. During the confrontation, the survivor's objective is to say what the he/she wants to say to the abuser and then leave.

A confrontation of this magnitude will be emotionally charged from start to finish. After the confrontation is over, the survivor may feel horrible or wonderful or at any of the points in-between. Any feelings she may have are perfectly understandable. Confrontations are frightening and painful and simultaneously provide an opportunity for the survivor to express her feelings, assert herself to the one who robbed her of her childhood and adulthood, and to feel empowered in front of the one person who made her feel so powerless. A feeling of relief is very common because there truly is no longer a secret. The last person has finally been confronted and told that the secret is out. As one survivor put it, "I had no idea that telling one more person could made such a difference. I had told practically everyone else little by little, but when I confronted my uncle I felt like I was suddenly free from the secret that had swallowed up my entire life."

After the confrontation, the most advantageous thing you can do to help the survivor is to be there to process what happened, to listen, comfort, celebrate, cry together. You have both worked hard together to reach this point. Take the time together now to feel proud of how far your loved one has come—from a victim in the grips of depression and nightmares to the person who stood up to her abuser as a survivor.

With all of these preparations and words of caution you may ask, "Why confront the perpetrator at all?" Some survivors feel a strong need to confront in order to put the issue truly at rest. While confrontation can be very traumatic, it offers many potential advantages for the survivor. In confronting the perpetrator, the survivor is doing what she wanted to have been able to do in the past; she is putting responsibility for the abuse where it belongs and, therefore is giving herself a message that it was not her fault.

In some cases, in order to prevent further abuse, public disclosure and legal confrontation within the courts may be necessary. Even in cases where legal authorities are not currently involved, if the statute cases where legal authorities are not currently involved, if the statute of limitations has not run out, the survivor may choose to prosecute the abuser. Prosecution often attaches meaning to the abuse experience by taking steps to prevent further abuse and may provide a symbolic retribution for the survivor in the form of a court ordered settlement to pay for therapy and other expenses.

It is ironic that some survivors may experience feelings of guilt about confronting the perpetrator because they consider the abuser's needs before their own. Assist the survivor to work through the guilt by reminding her she has a right to have her needs met and that it was the abuser who was responsible, not the survivor.

Not for everyone

Survivors should not be pressured into a confrontation. The choice must be theirs and theirs alone. For those who choose not to confront or cannot because the abuser is dead, there are alternatives to confrontation that often provide the same relief experienced by those who do confront. You and the survivor can let your imaginations run wild with ideas.

One woman whose abuser was dead made four banners, one for each week of the month, that said "Child Sexual Abuser" and each week she went to his grave and replaced the old banner with a fresh new one. She said "I don't think anyone ever saw me and few probably saw the banners, but I felt such relief knowing they were there to announce the truth and that finally the secret was out."

Another woman wrote an anonymous letter to the local paper about her abuse and warned others of the signs of child sexual abuse. The paper printed her letter. One survivor started a local support group for adult survivors, while another became heavily involved in state legislative processes where she told her story and lobbied for funds for the prevention of child sexual abuse. For each of these women, the activities they selected provided them with the sense of overwhelming relief that their secret was told, and some survivors gained a strong sense of added confidence and power through the selections they made.

There is no right or wrong way to put an end to the painful, burdensome secret of child sexual abuse carried by each survivor, but the secret must end. Help your loved one discover her own unique way to stomp out the final fragments of the secret she has carried far too long.

Especially for lovers

As the intimate partner of an adult survivor, you may have already encountered sexual difficulties in your relationship. Sexual responses may be distorted by the past experience of the abuse. Throughout the entire process of recovery, these difficulties may sometimes seem to broaden, intensify and grow in number. For some survivors this is the natural result of remembering and reexperiencing being abused while very young. This is a very sensitive issue for survivors and partners.

As your loved one moves through the healing process, intimacy may need to take on new forms to facilitate rather than to impede healing and to consider both of your needs. As the survivor's lover, the information presented in this book thus far has tried to provide you with the sensitivity to understand the emotional turmoil your lover/spouse is going through. You must also be sensitive to the changing sexual feelings of your loved one. Any sexual relationship with the abuse survivor requires understanding, commitment, communication and time if your sexual relations are to reach a point of mutual satisfaction.

The most abrupt changes in your sexual relationship are likely to occur in the remembering stage of early recovery. The survivor may be completely repulsed by the suggestion of love making, being unable to separate the present from the vivid images of the abuse being remembered. The sight of the genitals of the opposite sex may call forth all the feelings of fear and pain experienced as a small child. To be touched lovingly, even by her lover, may be too frightening for the survivor and cause her to pull violently away and dissolve into tears. This is a painful period of both of you. It is important to remember these actions are not directed toward you personally but result from an onslaught of memories. In childhood, sex and sexuality were associated with pain and powerlessness to the sexual abuse survivor, and this association is carried into the present by the recollection and reexperiencing of the abuse.

As a person recovers and learns to accept her feelings and her body's sensations, she may continue to hesitate to participate in something which for so long has been associated with mental and physical pain. It will take time to separate the survivor's current sexuality from her painful memories of the past.

For the survivor experiencing memories previously repressed, there is also little energy available for sex during the early stages of healing when the survivor's memories are returning with all of their intense feelings. After the discovery of the full extent of the abuse and its impact, there will eventually be a resurgence of interest in sex that is best explored slowly and with understanding.

Taking a respite from sexual relations may provide some survivors with the time needed to feel clear about what was then and what is now. An important healing element of the time out is that it enables the survivor to say no to sex when it is unwanted. For the child who was victimized and couldn't say "no," the survivor is empowered now by being able to say no and by having that decision respected by you, her partner.

In the early stages of healing, some survivors may only be able to have intercourse by shutting off their feelings and numbing their bodies—not exactly full participating partners in sex. If you truly respect and love your partner and want to have a lasting, satisfying sexual relationship in the future, you will not want to satisfy your own sexual need on an unresponsive body. Remember however, two people can be sexually intimate without having intercourse. Taking small steps toward intimacy agreeable to both lovers has the greatest probability of success, but any steps toward intimacy can be accompanied by the possibility of a negative outcome. Discuss alternatives with the survivor in a safe environment. It is often much easier for the survivor to discuss what is happening over a dining room table or in a quiet restaurant than in the bedroom.

Holding your partner and sharing intimate thoughts, kissing and gently caressing or massaging her, with her permission, may satisfy some of your intimate needs while allowing your lover the time and space to heal herself sexually. These small steps can provide the survivor with the opportunity to begin reexperiencing intimacy, slowly and gradually moving on to intercourse when she feels ready and comfortable. It is also helpful to discuss your intimacy and sexuality needs and find out what feels good for you and your partner, what doesn't feel right and what doesn't work, so together you can explore sexual activities that feel comfortable.

There may be a period of time when the survivor needs to be her own best lover. When all of her life's previously numbed feelings begin to emerge, your partner may experience sexual feelings she never realized before. Eager to explore these new sensations but still too frightened at the prospect of having a partner, she may turn to herself as her own lover. This is a natural and healthy choice and a wonderful opportunity to celebrate with your partner the important step forward in the healing process.

When your partner feels ready to explore sexual relations with you, the best advice is to take your time and both of you will reap the rewards. You remain the person she continues to love, but she may continue to experience some difficulty that only time and your understanding will overcome. You have a unique opportunity to explore what is best sexually for both of you, an opportunity few couples afford themselves unless confronted by a crisis. Proceed slowly, much like this is the very first time either of you have been sexually intimate. Agree beforehand to promise complete honesty and respect for each other and adhere to this promise. If something is distressing your partner while making love, make sure she knows that she can ask you to stop and that her wishes will be respected. Encourage her to talk to you about her feelings at this time. This will give the survivor a chance to slow down and connect with you. It will also help you feel more understanding of how her abuse is continuing to affect the two of you in the present. Discussing the fear is comforting and often the survivor will be ready to start sexual intimacy again after talking things over with you.

There may be times when your partner may experience frightening flashbacks while making love with you, envisioning an instant of the abuse. She may pull away, scream in terror or become very still. Any of these reactions are signs that the survivor is no longer in the present. Her reaction is to the past when the abuse occurred; it is not a reaction toward you. If this should happen, talk about what is going on. Ask what frightened her and if there are ways you can help her to remain in the present. Calling her name, reminding her it is you and not the abuser who is touching her is often helpful during these times. Sometimes a flashback will be so distressing that the survivor will choose not to continue sexual relations at the time. At other times talking about it will provide the comfort and security needed for her to continue.

If you can view yourselves as allies involved in solving the sexual difficulties you may encounter as the survivor continues to heal, you can avoid the hurt and frustration that may result from blaming each other for the problem. United, as mutually caring partners, you can meet each challenge and jointly find the way that is right for both of you and resume a life together in which sexual expression is an important element.

The following is a list of short guidelines which may help you and your loved one meet the sexual challenges that are the result of child sexual abuse.

- **Talk to each other.** Before, during and after sex, communicate openly to facilitate the building of a clear understanding for each other.
- **Don't take it personally.** The survivor's refusal to have sex or request to terminate sexual relations early are not about you. They are about the abuse and the abuser and it will require some time for the healing to be complete.
- **Don't blame your lover.** Remember that the difficulties are the abuser's fault, not the fault of the survivor.
- **Put yourself in the survivor's shoes.** Imagine the fears and concerns you would have as you begin your sexual relations all over again with the one you love, having full knowledge of the previously repressed child sexual abuse.
- **Validate your partner frequently.** Let your partner know that you will honor all her feelings that may arise around your sexual life together: anger, fear, frustration, desire, lack of desire.
- **Listen. Listen. Listen.** To meet the challenge of reestablishing sexual relations with the survivor you need to hear her concerns and feelings as you may never have before.
- **Provide reassurance.** Frequently reassure your partner that you are committed to her and to meeting and overcoming the challenges you are now facing together. Reassure her that you understand it will take time and that you're committing yourself to whatever time it will take.

Sexuality is an important component of each individual. The survivor's sexuality was taken away from her and used against her to inflict unbearable pain. The adult survivor struggles to reclaim her sexuality, the freedom to express it, and to experience the pleasure that sexual relations with a loved one can provide.

In helping a survivor through this experience you will undoubtedly confront feelings of anger, frustration, disappointment and even some despair within yourself. Stating otherwise would be untrue and unfair. Committing yourself to meeting the challenges as they arise and working through them with your partner promises a truly loving, sexual relationship of a quality that is obtained by few who have not been an active participant in the healing of a loved one.

Therapy

Having a professional therapist who is experienced in working with survivors and with whom the survivor can build a trusting relationship with is critical for healing the adult survivor. Friends, family members and lovers can't do it all alone, and the complexities of unresolved sexual abuse issues carried into adulthood are best sorted out a professional in this field. For many individuals, therapy, the therapeutic relationship and what goes on in therapy is shrouded in mystery and apprehension. These few pages are a brief attempt to remove some of the mystery and enable you to understand and be supportive of the survivor's therapy process.

Therapy has been known for years as the "talking cure" and maligned for just as many years by those who cannot see any value in talking about one's life for an hour each week with a stranger. In the early stages of therapy, the therapist, as a stranger, can be extremely beneficial to the survivor. He/she provides a totally nonjudgmental person to whom the survivor can tell anything without fear of rejection or reprisal. During this stage the therapist's job is one of data gathering—listening very carefully for both content and meaning in the story the survivor has to tell.

This is frequently a very difficult time for the survivor. She is being asked to break her silence one more time and tell her painful story to another person she does not know. Regardless of the level of empathy possessed by the therapist, the act of telling the survivor's story is very emotional. Some friends, family and lovers have questioned the helpfulness of therapy at this stage as they see their loved one go into therapy relatively composed and return afterward tearful and upset. While it is difficult to witness, the tears and accompanying emotions are of therapeutic value. They represent the out pouring of pain that accompanies the telling and retelling of the survivor's painful story of sexual abuse, a pain that is otherwise poisoning the survivor each day that it remains held captive inside.

The therapist will ask important questions of the survivor directed at unveiling memories that may have been inaccessible until now due to the defense mechanism of repression. These new recollections often cause substantial emotional distress for the survivor as she finds herself talking in detail about aspects of the abuse she was not consciously aware of before. It is the therapist's knowledgeable, well-placed questions, absent of any coercion, that allow the survivor's protective wall to lower and reveal more of the painful truth.

These early stages of therapy are very difficult for the survivor. If she appears very upset following therapy it may be helpful for you to accompany her to her appointments so she is not at risk when driving home afterward. She may or may not want to tell you about her therapeutic session. Try to understand the survivor's reluctance to speak about this. She is in the process of developing the special therapeutic relationship that will be very important, but one that is an adjunct, not a threat, to the relationship the two of you have together. Think of it as a sign of early progress that the survivor is struggling to develop her ability to trust again.

Explain your concern for the survivor and your need to know how to handle any potential crisis that may arise. Request the name and telephone number of the therapist so you can be in the best position to help the survivor if the need arises.

This also may be a good time for you to become acquainted with the therapist but only with the knowledge and approval of the survivor. A brief meeting is sufficient to introduce yourself and inquire how the therapist would handle a crisis situation, should one arise. Crises are most likely to arise during early stages of remembering. *Do not set up a meeting with the survivor's therapist without her approval.* This will only serve to undermine the survivor's trust in you and in the therapist, thereby jeopardizing therapy and the healing process.

Once the therapeutic relationship is well formed, the therapeutic task is turned toward making connections between the abuse and current maladaptive behaviors, thoughts and emotions of the survivor. This is the heart of therapy—where change begins to occur and healing becomes more apparent. The process is never easy or rapid and it cannot be rushed. It is at this point that the survivor is most likely to tell you what occurred at the therapy session, to share her new understandings with you and solicit your help in changing her old patterns. At times the survivor may just want you to listen. At other times she may ask you to play a more active role by pointing out particular behaviors or statements she makes that have become so automatic the survivor is unaware of them.

For some survivors, therapy may last longer than for others. The survivor may have more to remember, possess more behaviors that need modification, or need to move at a slower pace than others. There is no right pace. What is important is that the survivor maintains confidence in her therapist and is able to work with him/her as a team toward healthy change.

When the abuse was incest

The greatest percentage of child sexual abuse cases reported each year occur within the family of origin. The patterns and behaviors of incestuous families described here are only intended to help you understand the many issues that a survivor of incest has to heal as a result of the trauma of abuse itself and because the abuse took place within her family.

Abuse of power

Incest is always an abuse of power within the family. By definition, child sexual abuse is perpetrated by someone who occupies a position of power over the victim and uses that position to meet his/her own needs. The perpetrator exemplifies or sets the overall style for family interaction. In incestuous families the more powerful individuals abuse positions of power to meet their own needs without regard for the harm they cause to others, and this use of power becomes the norm for family interactions. Children in these families learn early that powerful people can make their own rules and change them without warning. As a result, children in incestuous families tend to see power exercised irresponsibly to meet the needs of the person in power, and the children may tend to model this behavior themselves.

Sometimes power is exercised by withdrawal. The powerful parent ignores or refuses to speak to one or all of the family members. Power may also be exercised by belittling others and their efforts by setting up situations in which the child is likely to fail. The overriding theme for the person in power is to meet his/her own needs first and to maintain control within a closed family system.

Fear of authority

Members of the incestuous family learn to fear authority. This is a fear that the authority of others will be destructive to themselves and their family. In addition, a sense of guilt about experiencing this fear is often experienced by the abused children. The guilt may be in fear of discovery of the incest secret and the consequences that may be experienced with disclosure. Fear of authority is largely dealt with by avoidance. When encounters with authority figures are unavoidable within the family, the child victim may exhibit a range of behaviors from passive to aggressive. Anxiety, suspicion, denial and hostility all may characterize the victim's behavior and are exacerbated within the family when a confrontation with the authority figure occurs or is anticipated.

Isolation

The incestuous family tends to be isolated and withdrawn from the rest of society. This closed family system constantly drains more and more energy from the individuals within the family and offers little positive energy in return. These families and their members develop few skills for healthy and effective coping with the outside world as a result of their isolation. The outside world is perceived as hostile and not to be trusted. Fear of authority is an important reason these families close themselves off from the outside world. Powerful members of the family discourage weaker members from establishing relationships with outsiders. Opportunities for children to form friendships and socialize away from the home are often limited or entirely forbidden. The incestuous parent often establishes himself as the sole linkage to the outside world ensuring his position of power, increasing the risk of abuse, and ensuring the secret of the abuse remains intact. This isolating pattern depletes the child's ability to establish resources of support and nurturing.

Denial

Denial is the major defense mechanism within the incestuous family and is frequently the only coping skill known to family members. Denial may actually be an extension of the secrecy phase of sexual abuse and even an expression of the secrecy itself. The incestuous family expends an enormous amount of energy on denial because the negative aspects of the family must be denied in order to be bearable. Family members routinely deny their feelings, especially when feeling angry, hurt, disappointed or frustrated, and the child victim learns very quickly how to integrate this behavior into her survival. Much of the denial is used to maintain a false image to the outside world that the incestuous home is a happy haven of security and freedom in comparison to the hostile outside world as perceived by the person in authority.

Maintaining isolation because the outside world is seen as hostile results in denial by family members of the positive and attractive aspects of the world outside of the incestuous family. Denial is useful in the short-run but requires increasing amounts of energy to maintain over time.

Lack of empathy

The inability to empathize with others is a hallmark of the perpetrator of incest. This characteristic includes an unresponsiveness to another's feelings and is rooted in denial and in a failure to communicate. It acts to simplify the abuse of power by the perpetrator because failure to perceive the negative consequences of exploitation of the child diminishes or eliminates guilt for the perpetrator.

Poor communication patterns

Members of the incestuous family generally do not develop the ability to communicate well with each other and, in turn, with outsiders. Interactions among family members are often characterized by acting out behavior and poor impulse control which serve as substitutes for direct verbal communication. No one within the family talks about what is really going on within the home. This family system fosters narcissistic, self-centered personalities. When children in these families are exploited by more powerful members, they learn that power and control are to be sought after and desired to avoid victimization in the future. The family's lack of communication combined with its isolation decreases the opportunities for its children to practice and develop healthy communication skills. This system, where poor communication is the norm, is often a source of great distress when the survivor discloses his/her secret as an adult and is met with denial and the refusal to listen and talk about the abuse by other family members.

Blurred boundaries

Incestuous families are often described as having no role boundaries. Family members typically behave in manners which are not in keeping with their appropriate roles of father, mother and child, frequently interchanging their roles. Inadequate controls and limit setting invite this blurring of role boundaries and results in role confusion for the young, vulnerable child. Physical boundaries are often ignored whenever the person of authority uses his power to observe or touch the child inappropriately and emotional boundaries blur when an adult turns to the child for gratification of his needs and roles become reversed.

The child victim in the incestuous family

Child victims of incest tend to have pervasive low self-esteem. Their sexual experiences within the family have left them feeling intense shame and guilt and their poor self-concept may be manifested in depression, withdrawal, and/or self-destructive behavior. Incest survivors may also exhibit a misleading facade of sophistication and maturity which masks the underlying childlike personality that has not been allowed to develop within the home. Since the child is dependent upon his/her parents for care and affection, as well as basic needs, child victims and adult survivors frequently experience intense ambivalence toward their parents and family system. This ambivalence is the result of the confusion the victims experience within the home. At times their needs may be met, especially their basic needs of food and clothing, leading them to view their family as warm and loving. At other times, however, the sexual abuse raises feelings the child has not learned to cope with: feelings of hurt, betrayal, confusion, and anger. These conflicting feelings are often dealt with by the child sliping into an ambivalent state as a means of self-protection.

In reality, the incestuous family is most often a "nonfamily" in a cultural sense. It is a group of individuals of varying ages, living under one roof and with a biological relationship to one another. However, the real ties between them are the sharing of interdependent dysfunctional behavior patterns developed as survival mechanisms rather than healthy, functional family relationships.

It is within the family system that children acquire their sense of identity, a sense of what is acceptable and unacceptable, knowledge of what it is to be a parent and a child, and how to communicate within the family unit and outside of it. For children of incest, all of these areas are blurred and confused and, as adult survivors, they require time to relearn these skills and heal from the faulty learning acquired in their family unit.

When incest occurs within the family, the entire family assumes a set of dynamics common to incestuous families. The following is a brief description of these common dynamics and their potential effect on the children in this kind of family.

- **Poor family boundaries.** There is little order among family members to delineate where one person ends and the other begins. There is little autonomy between members and therefore little individuality or privacy. Each child needs to develop a sense of his/her own separateness from those around him/her but in the incestuous family this is difficult if not impossible. This separateness allows for a sense of integrity, body, identity and assertiveness. When poor family boundaries exist this development is thwarted; the child has no sense of who he/she is apart from the family unit and has had no opportunity to practice asserting him/herself by saying "no."
- **Poor parental boundaries.** The children in these families exist to meet the needs of the parents rather than the parents being there to meet the needs of the children, as in a healthy family. With this dynamic in place, when the children are

used to meet the sexual needs of the parents, it is in accord with the overall belief system within the family.
- **Lack of effective parenting.** Children in these families are continually confused by inconsistencies between discipline and shows of affection with both frequently mixed. Disciplining the child typically involves shaming of him/her and the result is the development of low self-esteem on the part of the child.
- **Confusion about emotion and intimacy.** In these families it is common to see affection mixed with aggression or sexuality mixed with rage. Children within this environment have no opportunity to learn that this confusion is not a normal part of life and they internalize what they see and experience. If Daddy says he loves his little girl and then takes her to bed for sex, the child begins to associate all love with sex.

This is just a small list of incestuous family characteristics, but it is not difficult to see the long-term effects such an environment would have on a young, developing child who is being sexual abused within the family.

Family Dysfunction	Outcome
Poor family boundaries	No individuality
Poor sense of identity	Lack of assertiveness
Poor parental boundaries	Child is not allowed to be a child
	Child becomes sexual partner of parent
	Exaggerated need to please
Lack of effective parenting	Shame
Confusion between discipline /affection	Low self-esteem
Confusion of emotions /intimacy	Violence, aggression with affection
Closed family boundaries	Child never cries out for help
Withdrawal, isolation	

The goal of therapy and the healing process is to treat all of the effects of the incestuous family as well as the specific wounds inflicted by the sexual abuse itself. As difficult as healing may be for the incest survivor, once the family dynamics have been exposed in therapy, it becomes somewhat easier for the survivor to accept that the abuse was not her fault.

Sexually abused children from this type of family environment are likely to present themselves as adult survivors with numerous issues in addition to the abuse itself that require therapeutic care. Revealing the secret of the abuse is always difficult but coming from a home which placed great value on its closed system increases this difficulty. The survivor not only has to break the secret of the abuse but also has to break a family value learned since childhood. The child from the incestuous family grows into adulthood with these areas continuing to cause great pain and dysfunction.

Breaking the silence in the incestuous family is also particularly difficult because the survivor's siblings were raised in the same dysfunctional environment and may continue to carry on the old family belief system. If this is the case, the survivor will almost certainly meet with denial of her charges of abuse and experience rejection by family members. This is a very painful time for the survivor and she will need a great deal of support. Numerous studies have shown that regardless of the pain endured within the family, the majority of people still hold tightly to their need to belong and to be accepted by their family members. When the survivor's truth-telling results in angry, invalidating responses from other family members, this need to belong is shattered and the survivor may experience a crisis period at the loss of her family no matter how dysfunctional it was.

During this time it is important that
- The survivor not be alone;
- That she be helped to see the dysfunction lies within the family and not within her;
- That new relationships are begun to replace the lost family;
- The survivor should be encouraged to mourn her loss fully;
- The survivor views the family denial as a protective mechanism that has been in effect for a very long time.

In time, some family members may also come to recognize the family dysfunction, but in the immediate future the concern must be for the survivor who has broken the silence of her abuse. She needs your strong support and validation that the steps she has taken will lead to a healing of her old wounds. *The survivor needs your validation that regardless of the angry denials and rejections she may receive, that she is a worthwhile person, she has done nothing wrong, and that you are there for her.*

Some family members of the survivor report feelings of guilt upon hearing of the abuse that occurred within the family. Family members may experience a complex matrix of loyalty conflicts. They may be supportive of the survivor but then succumb to pressures from other family members to suppress or deny the reality, extent and/or effect of the sexual abuse. Both survivors and their supportive siblings often benefit from knowing that others have experienced the same mixed feelings. Siblings may experience survivor guilt, a deep regret and self-blame for not having been able to protect their sister/brother from the abuser. Just as survivors need to remind themselves that they were small, vulnerable children at the time of the abuse, siblings can be helped with the same reminders. They too were children and their guilt is unwarranted or unfair.

Siblings of the survivor may encounter another traumatic realization upon hearing of their sister's/brother's sexual abuse as a child. Siblings may or may not be consciously aware that they themselves sustained abuse within the family. You can help both the survivor and siblings by helping them find suitable professional help and support groups to address issues of suddenly remembered abuse triggered by hearing of the abuse of their sibling.

The split family

In some instances, when the survivor's secret has been revealed, the family may split into those who deny and reject and those who accept and believe the survivor. This may constitute both a positive and negative force for the survivor. Positively, survivors feel validated by those from within the family who truly know its characteristic structure and with whom they can partially fulfill their inner need to belong to a family. Negatively, survivors must decide what type of relationship to maintain with family members who do not accept and believe them.

You can assist the survivor in assessing her family relations by helping her answer the following questions for each family member
1. Does the survivor want to maintain this relationship or does it feel like more of an obligation?
2. What does the survivor receive from this relationship, what does she expected to give? Is it balanced?
3. How does the survivor feel after spending time with this person?
4. Does this person believe, listen and validate what the survivor has told him/her about the abuse and her current feelings?

Very careful consideration needs to be made when continuing relations within an incestuous family. A visit home can unleash the pent-up feelings of the small abused child that require days or weeks to recover from. Careful assessment will help the survivor make healthy decisions as an adult in the here and now rather than as a child still in search of the happy family that never was.

You can also encourage survivors to set ground rules with all family members they choose to continue a relationship with: What can or cannot be discussed, whether information the survivor discusses can be shared with other family members, whether contact will be in person or by telephone. The survivor has the right and is empowered when she sets forth these guidelines even though there is no guarantee that they will be honored. Taking this step is extremely frightening for the survivor initially because it goes contrary to the inner desire to be a part of an ideal family. Setting ground rules carries the risk that this dream family will be shattered forever. Remind her that her ideal family has never existed. An ideal family would not have allowed one of its children to be sexually abused by another of its members and have done nothing to protect that child. The small child could not say no to the abuser or set limits to protect herself from harm, but the adult survivor can and has the right to put her best interests first. This may be the first time that the survivor has insisted on what she needs within the family and she may experience feelings of guilt. Remind the survivor that she is important and her needs are important. Both deserve respect and support. If remaining in family relationships will undermine this basic integrity, then the cost of those relationships is too high for the well-being and future healthy relationships the survivor will enjoy.

When the abuser was a cleric

It has already been noted that the majority of child sexual abuse occurs within the family. Nonetheless a significant number of cases of child sexual abuse occur outside of the family, usually perpetrated by someone known and trusted by the child. The child sexual abuser may be a teacher, a scout master, a neighbor or a member of the clergy. Because of the growing number of reported cases of sexual abuse by clerics and because of features unique to this group of sexually abused children, this section intends to examine child sexual abuse in which the perpetrator was a cleric.

Archbishop John Roach of the Minneapolis-St.Paul Archdiocese wrote in the *St. Paul Pioneer Press Dispatch* in 1988, "Sexual abuse of a minor or vulnerable adult is a tragedy. The degree of the tragedy is heightened when the abuser is a priest, minister, teacher or anyone who occupies a privileged position in (the child's) relationship to the family."

Child sexual abuse is something nobody likes to talk about, but abuse by clerics has proven even more distasteful. With growing numbers of victims speaking out, each person must put aside his/her distaste long enough to look at the issues involved for the survivor. Only then can we be prepared to help a loved one who breaks the silence of the abuse and discloses that the abuser was a member of the clergy. All of the fundamental responses of the child and the long-term effects previously discussed also apply to children abused by clerics, but there are additional components which cause substantial damage to the victim distinctly different from those found in other forms of child sexual abuse.

Child sexual abuse by a cleric has many of the same dynamics as sexual abuse within the family. In most religious denominations the congregation is referred to and acts as a family system, secondary to the primary family system. There is a hierarchy of power between the cleric and parishioners much like that between the parents and children. The pastor, priest, rabbi or minister is revered as the head of this family and has a significant power bestowed upon him by his religion and sometimes by interpretations of scripture which demand reverence and obedience. Many people grew up believing clerics were holy men, next to God, to be feared, loved, obeyed.

When a child is sexually abused by a cleric, the losses are very much like those of a child abused by a parent but with some uniquely damaging aspects that require special help. The injuries sustained are spiritual as well as physical and emotional. Often his/her faith in God has been severely shaken. He/she may withdraw from all church activities which further isolates him/her and he/she may become distrustful of all clerics to the point that the mere sight of a clergy member causes severe fear and anxiety. In essence, the survivor challenges the very religion that has played a major role in shaping personal beliefs and values as the young boy or girl struggles to integrate religious teachings with the losses sustained at the time of the abuse.

Feelings of guilt and shame are common reactions for survivors and these feelings are particularly poignant for those victims who were sexually experienced at the time of the abuse. For victims who are abused by clerics there are additional feelings of guilt and shame stemming from religious teachings and from the abuser's threat to silence the child by combining religious dogma with the kinds of the threats used by other perpetrators of child sexual abuse. In addition to shame and guilt, survivors often experience substantial confusion over the abuse. Five psychologists involved in a Louisiana case of cleric child sexual abuse captured the nature of this confusion when they said, "Consider if you will, the impact on a child who is sexually abused by the cleric during the week, and on Sundays witnesses his/her parents bowing, kneeling, genuflecting, praying, receiving the sacraments and graciously thanking the priest (the abuser) for his involvement in their lives."[2]

Another source of confusion for certain victims comes from strict religious instruction that poorly delineates between rape or sexual violence—that may not be considered a sin *for the victim*—and other sexual activity outside of marriage—which can be viewed as a sin for anyone. The result of this vagueness too frequently leads the victim in this particular type of religion to view her victimization as a sexual sin for which she is responsible. These abused children are typically afflicted with guilt, confusion, humiliation, fear of rejection by their family and the loss of religious faith as the result of the sexual abuse by a clergy member.

Survivors often feel great ambivalence about the abuse because they have received benefits from the clergy member in the past. The church has been a place where the child has learned basic life values and a place to turn to for caring. With sexual abuse, the child has looked to a member of the clergy for faith and caring and has been met with betrayal.

Not only do clerics have easy access to children, they are authoritarian figures and often the objects of hero worship by the children. This may ease the road to seduction. The symbolic use the title "Father" in many religions and the Biblical commandment of "Honor thy father" puts victims in a state of great confusion and makes it easier for the perpetrator to take advantage of them.

Clerics who engage in the sexual abuse of children have betrayed the trust placed in them and have exploited the vulnerability of the child. This exploitation leaves the child feeling betrayed by the cleric, the church and by God.

If you are a religious person, your first instinct may be to encourage survivors to find peace and strength through prayer and by attending church services. Your instincts may be honorable but they are likely to be met with disastrous results. *Remember that survivors often feel betrayed not only by one clergy member but also by the church and by God.* All three can trigger the emotional pain of the past and continue to cause intense pain today. If survivors are to ever involve themselves in religious activities again, it will take time and it needs to occur only when they are ready to do so. Don't push them.

If you are very emotionally involved with the survivor, she may view *your* continued participation in the church as a personal betrayal of her and all she's had to suffer due to the abuse.

> *Sharon felt hurt and outrage that her friend did not immediately cease her involvement in the church when she learned of Sharon's abuse. "I thought if she cared about me at all she would have stopped going to that awful place."*

You must make your own decisions to take care of yourself while helping the adult survivor. Seeing the survivor's pain, you may be tempted to comply with her wishes or you may tell her that you have complied and then continue your religious practices in secret. Neither is a viable alternative. Both pose a substantial risk to your relationship. Truthfulness is always best. Discuss your spiritual needs with the survivor and emphasize that your continued participation does not invalidate the pain of her experience. You might make clear to the survivor that you feel the particular cleric-abuser is to blame for her feelings, not the entire religion. It is possible for you to remain active in your church and still share in the pain and outrage of the sexual abuse perpetrated upon the survivor. You may even find that your unique role motivates you to become actively involved in your church to insure that it has methods of prevention, intervention and treatment for both the survivors and perpetrators of sexual abuse.

Confrontation in abuse by a member of the clergy

Churches have been very slow in responding to the problem of sexual abuse by clerics. Slowly they have begun to institute policies, procedures and the appointment of committees and specific individuals to address the problem of sexual abuse wherever it arises. While some church officials are becoming increasingly more accessible to survivors who wish to confront the church and to file a grievance, others remain unresponsive and defensive.

Confronting the church is not unlike confronting an individual abuser. The exception is that confronting a church involves more people within a large, often intimidating institution. It's important to remember that the church is made up of individual women and men, rather than one powerful entity. On the positive side of such a confrontation is the increasing likelihood that the church has policies and procedures for dealing with sexual abuse already in place, unlike any response in confronting the lone abuser.

Whenever the intent is to confront a large institution, the best course of action is to be well prepared. Questions to help the survivor determine what the goals of the confrontation are

- Is the confrontation informative or is some action desired?

- Is the intent to have the abusing cleric removed from the church; committed into treatment; or to be allowed to continue his ministry with strict restrictions?
- Does the survivor desire compensation for his/her therapeutic costs?
- Is a public notification naming the perpetrator to the congregation desired?

Assist the survivor to answer these and other relevant questions you both may think of to arrive at an agenda for the meeting with church officials. Remember, this is the survivor's meeting and agenda; be prepared. The policies and procedures for handling victims and perpetrators developed by the church should be of public record and reviewing them may be useful to you at this point to prepare for the confrontation.

When the agenda for the meeting has been established, it is time to schedule an appointment with the appropriate church officials. This may be very frightening for the survivor. If the survivor desires, offer to take this step with him/her. Schedule a time when you both can go together. You can act as moral support and be right there to process what happened at the meeting when it is completed. This should be expected to be a very emotional time for survivors as they have to tell their secret once again, face-to-face with those who represent the abuser. Don't leave them alone afterward. They will need some time with you as both a support person and one to provide them with a feeling of protection. The meeting itself will likely trigger very painful memories of the abuse. If the meeting leaves the survivor feeling unimportant and invalidated, at the worst, he/she may experience suicidal thoughts and will need to have you there for intervention.

It is important to know that confronting the church and even getting all of the items the survivor has requested does not end the process of pain and healing that he/she will continue to face. What it does accomplish for some is a renewed sense of validation and empowerment, both of which are integral to the healing process.

Legal action may be the only means to receive validation and compensation for survivors. Justice Francis T. Murphy, in a speech on child sexual abuse in 1985 said, "Children have neither power or property. Voices other than their own must speak for them. If those voices are silent, then children who have been abused may lean their heads against window panes and taste the bitter emptiness of violated childhoods."[3]

Recovery?—recovered?—resolution!

It may be clear to you at this point that there is an obvious absence of the words "recovery" or "recovered" within these pages. This was intentional. We could ask, "Which words describe the child sexual abuse healing process?" Before answering, it is important to clarify what each of these three words mean within our language. Webster's New Universal Unabridged Dictionary, Deluxe Second Edition, 1983 provides the following definitions.

Recovered is
> To regain after losing, retrieve
> To regain health, composure, etc.

Recovery is
> The act or process of recovering

Resolution is
> The act of resolving, to decide or determine, to make clear, explain or solve a problem.

For many friends, family members or lovers the question is how and when will they know that the trauma is over, that their loved one has now moved on from recovery to being recovered? Keeping each of the above definitions in mind, I'll first explore "recovery" vs. "recovered" and later move on in an attempt to clarify and answer this very common concern.

For adult survivors of child sexual abuse with professional and even non-professional help, support and care, it is highly probable that they will regain their health and composure. In this interpretation of the word, they will be recovered. The severe depression with its suicidal thoughts will be a thing of the pas. The nightmares will be no more frequent than those of other sleepers. Patterns of excessive sleep or insomnia will return to healthy night's sleep. Episodes of crippling anxiety and explosive rage will be reduced to typical anxiety and healthy anger. Eating disorders will be replaced with a healthy appetite and body image resulting in a healthy appearance. According to the second definition of "recovered," the survivors have recovered.

The first segment of the definition, "to regain after losing," is also applicable to physical health issues of survivors, however, in the wider scope of losses incurred as a result of the child sexual abuse, survivors have not, nor can they ever recover. It is possible to travel back in time and regain the lost memories and feelings of the sexual abuse that have been repressed from conscious awareness for years. It is also possible to regain a sense of meaning those events have had on their lives since the abuse occurred. This can affect positive changes in the present and for the future. It is not possible to regain, (recover) that which was lost during all of the time since the abuse. The lost childhood with its innocence and trust cannot be regained or fully restored to its original form. There are the parts of a life that do not remain frozen until recovered but are fluid, constantly undergoing changes, rendering them incapable of being recovered. If this argument is valid, survivors can recover in part—their health and composure—but cannot recover all that has been lost as a result of the abuse.

This would initially appear to paint a bleak picture for the survivor were it not for the word "recovery, the striving to regain what was lost." To strive is to seek and to be hopeful. While all that was lost to the child abuse victim cannot be recovered, it can be sought after throughout life and those pieces regained can be incorporated into the present. As the healing continues, so does recovery, with each passing day strengthening both what has been recovered and that which continues to be sought after. To be recovered is a final, stagnant concept that tends to say "All is right" at a given point in time. Recovery is a dynamic, fluid process of daily change and discovery of the self. For the child sexual abuse survivor it is "recovery" rather than being "recovered" that is the objective for life once past the abuse.

Adult child sexual abuse survivors will not be recovered once they have gone through the healing process but that is not something to be sorrowful for. Instead, through the horrible events of their childhood and the painful healing process, that has brought them to a level of higher self-awareness, they are recovering for life. For survivors, it is a process of continuing personal enrichment and growth; a process of integrating their past into their present to create their very own unique future. This is cause for celebration. It depicts the human condition common to all of us. Everyone is recovering from prior wounds; it is the on-going process of growth. Adult survivors will continue to recover throughout life but due to the healing process they have experienced, recovery will not continue to be ridden with crisis and indescribable pain. Recovery will be a process of living each day to the fullest despite everything that has come before.

Resolution overlaps the latter stages of recovery as survivors are now able to make clear, explain, and solve many of the issues surrounding their abuse and its impact upon their life. It is in resolution that survivors can make clear that the abuse was not their fault. They can explain many problems they've experienced in life as a result of the abuse and are able to utilize all of this information to determine for themselves how they will proceed with their lives.

Resolution is an informed, determined choice that comes from deep within the survivor's newly discovered sense of self. Resolution must come from within the survivor; it cannot be pressured from the outside. As a friend, family member or lover, you want very much for your loved one to be well again, but no one possesses this desire more than the survivor. Resolution pressured from the outside is never authentic and as such doesn't last long.

The following signs will help you determine when resolution has begun for your loved one:

- **The survivor's feelings and perspectives begin to stabilize.** The mood swings slow, the survivor has developed a much clearer sense of what she is feeling rather than emotionally numbing herself, and perspectives on life include a future of possibilities rather than dark despair.
- **The survivor now affirms the strengths she has developed.** There is an increase in self-esteem that now allows strengths as well as weaknesses to be acknowledged. The appearance and affirmation of strengths are milestones for survivors who have seen themselves as bad, inadequate and powerless.
- **The survivor recognizes her resiliency.** Once enmeshed in the abuse, feeling like she would never see her way past it, the survivor now begins to realize that she *is* getting past it. Recalling the early stages of remembering, the survivor can now see how her resiliency has helped to bring her through

and will continue to work as an asset as she faces new challenges.
- **The survivor begins to stand up for her own truths.** The small child unable to stand up for herself and the bruised adult still trying to please others gives away to an adult who is aware of her truths and is now feeling rightly empowered to stand up for and defend those truths.
- **A drive to be healthy appears.** The survivor may show an increased interest in socializing with others, desire for healthy exercise, eating disorders slowly fade and sleep is normalized. All of these reflect a renewed concern on the part of the survivor for her health.
- **The survivor changes her view of personal power and the power of others.** In resolution, the survivor is able to understand and begin to undertake the processes of change that are within her power. At the same time, she recognizes those things she does not have the power to change and begins the process of letting these things go.
- **The survivor begins to see herself as a whole, rather than a compartmentalized person.** The small abused child and adult person become integrated as one through the healing process, resulting in a whole person of which the abuse is only one part.
- **Life becomes more than a reaction to the abuse.** All of these signs of resolution come together and the survivor is now involved in living all aspects of life. She is no longer dominated by the thoughts, feelings and fears of the abuse. The abuse remains a presence in her life but all of life's actions or inactions are no longer a reaction to the abuse. Each experience begins to stand on its own merit with the abuse more of a backdrop to the actions of life than the director.

The survivor will be recovering for the rest of her life. The events of the past abuse cannot be eradicated nor can the losses experienced be fully recovered, thus the survivor remains on a continuum of recovery. There is no shame or guilt to be "recovering." In a very real sense, recovery is the art of living and all forms and stages of the on-going recovery should be celebrations of the survivor's spirit to merely survive at first, then to survive with some conviction, and finally to survive and flourish.

Reaching this final stage, celebrate what you and your loved one have gone through and shared together. The growth each of you have experienced is a result of being part of this process. You are both very different people as a result of your sharing in the healing process and have a very special bond with each other that few will ever get the opportunity to develop. It is a bond you can carry with you for the rest of your life. As the friend, family member or lover, you have played an important role in the healing of another precious life, and now, after the turbulent times have passed, you can look upon your loved one and take pride in knowing that you contributed to making this recovery possible when initially the survivor could feel only hopelessness.

You may recognize some of the above discussion of recovery and a continued lifetime of recovery as a common element of the Alcoholics Anonymous program. It is true, the survivor and the recovering alcoholic do have these things in common, and Alcoholics Anonymous has a wonderful tradition that you and your loved one may want to consider for yourselves. In AA when someone has reached year-long sobriety, there is a celebration to honor that achievement. It doesn't end there. For each subsequent year of sobriety a celebration and acknowledgment of the alcoholic's on-going successful recovery is held.

You and your survivor may want to begin a similar tradition—the celebration of being a survivor of child sexual abuse and no longer a victim—and the celebration of your increased love and respect for each other for having shared in undertaking this difficult journey of healing.

Footnotes

[1] Fortune, Marie, *Is Nothing Sacred?* (1989) Harper & Row, New York, NY.

[2] *National Catholic Reporter*, "Priest Child Abuse Cases Victimizing Families; Bishops Lack Policy Response," 1985

[3] Hechler, D., *The Battle and the Backlash*, Lexington Books, Lexington, MA., 1988

References

Books:

Barnes, Patty Derosier, *The Woman Inside, from Incest Victim to Survivor,* (1989), Mother Courage Press, Racine, WI.

Bass, Ellen, and Davis, Laura, *The Courage to Heal,* (1988), Harper and Row, New York, NY.

Baxter, Arlene, *Techniques for Dealing with Child Sexual Abuse,* (1986), Basic Books, New York, NY.

Butler, Sandra, *Conspiracy of Silence: The Trauma of Incest* (1985), Volcano Press, Volcano, CA.

Credson, J., *By Silence Betrayed: Sexual Abuse of Children in America,* (1988), Little Brown and Company, Boston, MA.

Daugherty, Lynn B., Ph.D., *Why Me? Help for Victims of Child Sexual Abuse (Even If They Are Adults Now),* (1984), Mother Courage Press, Racine, WI.

Dolan, Yvonne, M., *Resolving Sexual Abuse,* (1951), W.W. Norton & Company, New York, NY.

Figley, C.R., *Trauma and Its Wake: The Study and Treatment of Post Traumatic Stress Disorder,* (1984), Brunner-Mazel, New York, NY.

Figley, C.R., *Trauma and Its Wake: Vol II - Post Traumatic Stress Theory, Research and Intervention,* (1985), Brunner-Mazel, New York, NY.

Finkelhor, David, *A Sourcebook on Child Sexual Abuse*, (1986), Sage Publications, Beverly Hills, CA.

Finkelhor, David, *Sexually Victimized Children*, (1987), New York Free Press, New York, NY.

Fortune, Marie, *Is Nothing Sacred?* (1989), Harper & Row, New York, NY.

Fortune, Marie, *Keeping the Faith*, (1987), Harper & Row, New York, NY.

Fortune, Marie, *Sexual Violence: The Unmentionable Sin, an Ethical and Pastoral Perspective*, (1983), The Pilgrim Press, New York, N.Y.

Gil, Eliana, Ph.D., *Outgrowing the Pain*, (1984), Launch Press, CA.

Graber, Ken, M.A., *Ghosts in the Bedroom*, (1991), Health Communications, Inc., Deerfield Beach, FL.

Hechler, D., *The Battle and the Backlash*, (1988), Lexington Books, Lexington, MA.

Herman, Judith Lewis, *Father-Daughter Incest*, (1981) Harvard University Press, Cambridge, MA.

Justice, B., and Justic, R., *The Broken Taboo: Sex in the Family*, (1979) Human Services Press, New York, NY.

Kempe, R., and Kempe, C.H., *The Common Secret: Sexual Abuse of Children and Adolescents* (1988). Freeman and Co., New York, NY.

Maltz, Wendy, *Incest and Sexuality: A Guide to Understanding and Healing*, (1987), Lexington Books, Lexington, MA.

Mayer, Adele, *Sexual Abuse: Causes, Consequences and Treatment*, (1985), Learning Publications, Holmes Beach, Fl.

Meiselman, Karen C., *Incest: A Psychological Study of Causes and Effects,* (1978), Jossey-Bass Publications, San Francisco, CA.

Middleton-Moz, Jane, *Children of Trauma*, (1989), Health Communications, Inc., Deerfield Beach, FL.

Miller, Alice, *The Drama of the Gifted Child*, (1981) Basic Books, Inc., New York, NY.

Miller, Alice, *Thou Shalt Not Be Aware: Society's Betrayal of the Child*, (1986), New American Library, Ontario, Canada.

Miller, Ann, *Pictures of a Childhood,* (1986), Farrar, Strause, Giroux, New York, NY.

Minnesota Department of Corrections, *Incest: Confronting the Silent Crime*, (1982), Minnesota Program for Victims of Sexual Abuse.

Mrazek, Patricia Beezley, and C. Henry Kempe, *Sexually Abused Children and Their Families*, (1981), Permagon Press, Inc., Tarrytown, NY.

Pynoss, R., and E. S., *Post Traumatic Stress Disorder*, (1985), Psychiatric Press, Washington, DC.

Quina, Kathryn, and Carlson, Nancy L., *Rape, Incest and Sexual Harassment: A Guide for Helping Survivors*, (1989), Prager, N.Y.

Renshaw, Domeena C., *Incest: Understanding and Treatment*, (1982), Little Brown Publishing, Boston, MA.

Russel, Dianna E.H., *The Secret Trauma: Incest in the Lives of Girls and Women*, (1986), Basic Books, New York, NY.

Rutter, Peter, M.D., *Sex in the Forbidden Zone*, (1989) Jeremy P. Tarcher, Inc., Los Angeles, CA.

Schoener, G.R., Milgrom, J.H, Gonsiorek, J.C., Luepker, E.T, Conroe, R.M., *Psychotherapists' Sexual Involvement with Clients*, (1990), Walk-In Counseling Center, Minneapolis, MN.

Segal, Julius, and Yahraes, Herbert, *A Child's Journey*, (1978), McGraw-Hill Book Company, New York, NY.

Sgori, Suzanne M., M.D., *Vulnerable Populations: Evaluations and Treatment of Sexually Abused Children and Adult Survivors, Vol 1*, (1988), Lexington Books, Lexington, MA.

Sgori, Suzanne M., M.D., *Vulnerable Populations: Evaluations and Treatment of Sexually Abused Children and Adult Survivors, Vol 2*, (1988) Lexington Books, Lexington, MA.

Sgroi, Suzanne, *Handbook of Clinical Intervention in Child Sexual Abuse*, (1982), Lexington Books, Lexington, MA.

Strouse, Evelyn, *Incest: Family Problems Community Concern*, (1985), Public Affairs Committee, New York, NY.

Vander Mey, Brenda, and Ronald L. Neff, *Incest as Child Abuse*, (1986), Praeger, New York, NY.

Whitfield, Charles, L., M.D., *Healing the Child Within*, (1987), Health Communications, Inc., Deerfield Beach, FL.

Publications/Periodicals

Alexander, Pamela C., and Shirley L. Lupfer, "Family Characteristics and Long-Term Consequences Associated with Sexual Abuse," *Archives of Sexual Behavior*, Vol. 16, No. 3.

American Humane Association, *Model of Child Sexual Abuse Outcomes* (1984), Denver, Colorado.

Conte, J.R., *A Look at Child Sexual Abuse*, (1989) #232, National Committee for Prevention of Child Abuse.

Elwell, M.E., "Sexually Assaulted Children and Their Families," *Social Casework*, Vol 60, 227-235, 1979.

Fatout, M.F. "Consequences of Abuse on Relationships of Children," *Families in Society*, Vol 71, No 2, 1990.

Finkelhor, D., and Brown, A., "The Traumatic Impact of Child Sexual Abuse," *The American Journal of Orthopsychiatry*, 1985.

Helfer, "Looking at Outcomes," *Child Abuse and Neglect,* Vol 10:277-395, 1986.

Herman, J, and Hirschman, L., "Incest Between Fathers and Daughters," *The Sciences*, Oct., 1977, pp.4-7.

"Post Traumatic Stress Disorder," *Journal of American Academy of Child & Adolescent Psychiatry*, Vol. 27:645-54, Sept. 1988.

"The Long Term Effects of Child Sexual Abuse," *Journal of Consulting Clinical Psychology*, Vol 56:5-8, Fall, 1988.

Lutsig, N., J.W. Dresser, S.W. Spellman, T.B. Murray, "Incest: A Family Group Survival Pattern," *Archives of General Psychiatry* 14:31:40, 1966.

Nakashima, Ida and Gloria Zakus, "Incest: A Review and Clinical Experience," *Pediatrics* 60:696-701 (November, 1977).

"Priest Child Abuse Cases Victimizing Families, Bishops Lack Policy Response," *National Catholic Reporter*, 1985, A-1.

Basic Facts about Child Sexual Abuse, National Committee for Prevention of Child Abuse, (1987).

"Archbishop Explains Diocesan Policies to Combat Sexual Abuse," *St. Paul Pioneer Press Dispatch*, 1988.

Silver, R.L., Boon, C., and Stones, M.H. (1983) "Searching for Meaning in Misfortune: Making Sense of Incest," *Journal of Social Issues*, 39, 81-102.

Spelman, C., *Talking about Child Sexual Abuse,* (1989), #232, National Committee for Prevention of Child Abuse.

Spinetta, John J., and David Rigler, "The Child Abusing Parents," *Psychological Bulletin*, Vol. 77, No 4:296-304, 1972.

Summit, Roland, and Kryso, "Sexual Abuse of Children: A Clinical Spectrum," *American Journal of Orthopsychiatry,* 48:237-51, 1978.

Taylor, J.W., "The Use of Nonverbal Expression with Incestuous Clients," *Families in Society*, Vol. 71, No 10, 1990.

It's Never O.K., The Task Force on Sexual Exploitation by Counselors and Therapists, (1988), Minnesota Department of Corrections, St. Paul, MN.

# Mother Courage Press

In addition to *Helping the Adult Survivor of Child Sexual Abuse, for Friends, Family and Lovers*, Mother Courage publishes the following titles.

Self-Help, Sexual Abuse, Prevention

Why Me? Help for victims of child sexual abuse, even if they are adults now by Lynn B. Daugherty, Ph.D. Important and informative book for beginning the process of healing the psychological wounds of child sexual abuse. Paper $7.95

Something Happened to Me by Phyllis E. Sweet, M.S. Sensitive, straightforward book designed to help children victimized by sexual or other abuse. Paper $4.95

The Woman Inside, from Incest Victim to Survivor by Patty Derosier Barnes. This workbook is designed to help an incest victim work through pain, confusion and hurt. Paper $11.95

Warning! Dating may be hazardous to your health! by Claudette McShane. Date rape and dating abuse study emphasizes that women need not put up with any kind of abuse, are not to blame for being abused and can regain control of their lives. Paper $9.95

Fear or Freedom, a Woman's Options in Social Survival and Physical Defense by Susan E. Smith. This book realistically offers options to fear of social intimidation and fear of violent crime with an important new approach to self-defense for women. Paper $11.95

I Couldn't Cry When Daddy Died by Iris Galey. Courageous and sensitive personal account of an incest survivor. Story of inspiration and hope. Paper $9.95

Rebirth of Power, Overcoming the Effects of Sexual Abuse through the Experiences of Others, edited by Pamela Portwood, Michele Gorcey and Peggy Sanders, is a powerful and empowering anthology of poetry and prose by survivors of sexual abuse. Paper $9.95

Healing Spells for Sexually Betrayed Women, by Sue Silvermarie. Healing through moving dramatic poetry and through suggestions for visualization and meditation. Paper $8.95

Travel Adventure

Women at the Helm by Jeannine Talley. Two women sell everything and begin an adventure-filled cruise around the world in a 34-foot sailboat. Paper $11.95, Hardcover $19.95

Banshee's Women, Capsized in the Coral Sea by Jeannine Talley. Continuing adventures of Talley and Smith as they are capsized and dismasted off the east coast of Australia. Paper $12.95, Hardcover $21.95

Biography

Olympia Brown, The Battle for Equality by Charlotte Coté. Biography of an unsung foremother, talented orator and the first ordained woman minister in the US who fought a life-long battle for equal rights for women. Paper $9.95, Hardcover $16.95

Humor

Womb with Views, A Contradictionary of the Enguish Language by Kate Musgrave is a delightful, more than occasionally outrageous social commentary cartoon-illustrated feminist dictionary. Paper $8.95

New Age

Welcome to the Home of Your Heart by Dorothy "Mike" Brinkman. Messages of universal love, caring and compassion given to Brinkman by an entity named Jenny. Paper $11.95

Meditations and Blessings from a Different Dimension by Dorothy "Mike" Brinkman. A healing book of channeled meditations and blessings taken from *Welcome to the Home of Your Heart*. Paper $5.95

Woman Studies/Lesbian

NEWS by Heather Conrad is a gripping novel of a women's computer takeover to make the empire builders and the money makers stop destroying the people and the earth. Paper $9.95

Night Lights by Bonnie Shrewsbury Arthur. More than your traditional lesbian romance, this novel tackles various issues—with a light touch that will make you laugh out loud. Paper $8.95

Singin' the Sun Up by Ocala Wings. Communicating with dolphins gives this lesbian love story a New Age twist. Paper $8.95

Mega by B. L. Holmes. Science fiction lesbian romance set against a future of giant cities and vast pollution of the Earth. Paper $8.95

Hodag Winter by Deborah Wiese. A first grade teacher is fired for being a lesbian. She and her lover and friends fight the action. Paper $8.95

Rowdy & Laughing by B. L. Holmes. She's not gay, she's rowdy and laughing. Poems encompass the joy of life and being in love. Paper $4.95

Senior Citizen by B. L. Holmes. A musical comedy, this funny and touching play explores the dual themes of rejection of the aged, gays and lesbians. Paper $8.95

And Then I Met This Woman, Previously Married Women's Journeys into Lesbian Relationships by Barbee Cassingham and Sally O'Neil. A collection of 36 stories of women who were married and then fell in love with another woman. Paper $9.95

If you don't find these books in your local book store, you may order them directly from Mother Courage Press at 1533 Illinois Street, Racine, WI 53405. Please add $3 for postage and handling for the first book and 50¢ for each additional book.